COMPLEX SYSTEMS

Minds·On PHYSICS

Activities & Reader

COMPLEX SYSTEMS

Minds·On
PHYSICS

Activities & Reader

William J. Leonard
Robert J. Dufresne
William J. Gerace
Jose P. Mestre

The University of Massachusetts
Physics Education Research Group

 KENDALL/HUNT PUBLISHING COMPANY
4050 Westmark Drive   Dubuque, Iowa 52002

Also available in the Minds•On Physics Series

Minds•On Physics: Motion / Activities & Reader

Teacher's Guide to accompany Minds•On Physics: Motion

Minds•On Physics: Interactions / Activities & Reader

Teacher's Guide to accompany Minds•On Physics: Interactions

Minds•On Physics: Conservation Laws & Concept-Based Problem Solving / Activities & Reader

Teacher's Guide to accompany Minds•On Physics: Conservation Laws & Concept-Based Problem Solving

Minds•On Physics: Fundamental Forces & Fields / Activities & Reader

Teacher's Guide to accompany Minds•On Physics: Fundamental Forces & Fields

Teacher's Guide to accompany Minds•On Physics: Complex Systems

Minds•On Physics: Advanced Topics in Mechanics / Activities & Reader

Teacher's Guide to accompany Minds•On Physics: Advanced Topics in Mechanics

Author Address for Correspondence

William J. Leonard
Department of Physics
Box 34525
University of Massachusetts
Amherst, MA 01003–4525 USA

e-mail: WJLEONARD@physics.umass.edu

Cover Photos: Image of roller coaster "The Dragon" courtesy of Adventureland Park, Des Moines, Iowa. Tennis player image © 1997 PhotoDisc. All other images courtesy of Corel.

ISBN 0-7872-5413-4

This book was prepared with the support of NSF Grant: ESI 9255713. However, any opinions, findings, conclusions and or recommendations herein are those of the authors and do not necessarily reflect the views of NSF.

Printed in the United States of America
10 9 8 7 6 5 4 3 2 1

Contents

How to Use this Book   xiii

Acknowledgments   xv

Activities

continued

Activities (continued)

Reader
COMPLEX SYSTEMS

CHAPTER 1. Fluids

Reader (continued)

1.1 DENSITY AND PRESSURE   *R1–6*

1.1.1 Density   *R2*

▶ definition of *density*   *R2*

▶ symbol for density is ρ *R2*

▶ units of density are kg/m^3 or g/cm^3 *R2*

▶ examples using a nickel and a baseball   *R2*

▶ density is <u>not</u> a measure of how "thick" a fluid is   *R2*

1.1.2 Dependence of density on location or circumstances   *R2–4*

▶ density does not generally depend on how much of a substance you have   *R2,3*

▶ some volume conversions (gal, qt, L, and cm^3)   *R3*

▶ gases have mass and weight   *R3*

▶ density can depend on conditions, such as varying temperature and pressure   *R3*

▶ definition of *incompressible*   *R4*

1.1.3 Distinguishing mass, weight, and density   *R4*

▶ definitions of *mass*, *weight*, and *density*   *R4*

▶ examples that demonstrate the differences between mass, weight, and density   *R4*

1.1.4 Pressure   *R5,6*

▶ definition of *pressure*   *R5*

▶ what is meant by *planar*   *R5*

▶ the pressure in the atmosphere at the surface of the Earth is about 10N/cm^2 *R5*

▶ comparison of the forces exerted by air on two cereal boxes   *R5*

▶ pressure is not a force   *R5*

▶ why the cereal boxes are not crushed by the forces exerted by air   *R6*

▶ direction of the force exerted by a fluid depends on the orientation of the surface   *R6*

▶ why there must be air underneath an object even when it is sitting on a table   *R6*

▶ suction cups are different; there is little or no air beneath them   *R6*

continued

Reader (continued)

Reader (continued)

continued

Reader (continued)

Reader (continued)

continued

Reader (continued)

Reader (continued)

continued

Reader (continued)

Reader (continued)

How to Use this Book

The activities in this book are designed to get you *thinking about* and *doing* physics—in a way that is a lot closer to the way professional scientists think about and do science. You will learn by communicating your ideas with your teacher and with other students, and by trying to make sense of the ideas presented in the book.

During the school year, you may be required to memorize some definitions, vocabulary, and other basic information, but you should <u>not</u> try to memorize the answers to specific questions and problems. Answers should *make sense to you*. If they do not make sense to you, then you probably should go back and change how you think about the problem or situation. Even if everyone else seems to understand something, please do not give up! Keep trying until it makes sense to you.

We want *everyone* in the class to understand physics, and we sincerely believe that everyone *can* learn to understand physics, because the activities are designed to help everyone develop the skills needed to learn physics. If necessary, your teacher and your classmates should be able to help you. Find out how they think about a problem or situation, and adapt their ideas to your own way of thinking. And if you are helping someone else, remember that everyone learns at a different rate, so please be patient.

This style of learning requires a lot of dedication and work, especially if you are not familiar with the style. In the short run, this style might seem impossible and not worth the extra effort. But in the long run, it is definitely worth it. We really, really want you to memorize *as little as possible*. Focus on the ideas that are most widely useful, and learn how to use these to derive the relationships you might need to answer a question or solve a problem. You will be able to solve lots of problems using this approach, and you will develop skills that will be useful in any field you might choose to enter. Remember that physics is one way—among many—of looking at the natural world. It's a way of analyzing, evaluating, describing, explaining, and predicting the behavior of objects and collections of objects.

Acknowledgments

The *concept-based problem-solving* approach to learning is the way Bill Gerace has taught hundreds of graduate and undergraduate students at the University of Massachusetts. It is his approach that has been refined, modified, and adapted to create the activities in this book.

We are deeply grateful to the National Science Foundation for funding the pilot project, *Materials for Developing Concept-Based Problem-Solving Skills in Physics*, under grant MDR–9050213. Although we had no prior experience writing materials for high-school physics, the Foundation reasoned that as experts in both physics and cognitive research, we were uniquely qualified to bring a fresh outlook to the task. We thank NSF also for funding the renewal, *Minds-On Physics: An Integrated Curriculum for Developing Concept-Based Problem Solving in Physics*, under grant ESI–9255713. The materials in this book are a direct result of this funding and are also evidence of how federal support can impact education and stimulate reform. We thank Gerhard Salinger, our project director at NSF, for his unwavering support of our approach and his many suggestions.

We are very fortunate to have found four wonderful teachers who were willing to try a different approach to teaching physics by field-testing those first 24 "modules" of the pilot project: Charlie Camp (Amherst Regional HS, Amherst, MA), Mike Cunha (Weaver HS, Hartford, CT), Steve Degon (Central HS, Springfield, MA) and Hughes Pack (Northfield–Mount Hermon School, Northfield, MA). They let us into their classrooms and let us see first-hand how their students dealt with the approach. Their numerous suggestions have improved the materials and the approach greatly.

We also thank all the teachers who have field-tested Minds•On Physics activities: Jane Barrett (Howard School of Academics & Technology, Chattanooga, TN), Larry Blanchard (Warren Easton HS, New Orleans, LA), Roger Blough (Tyner HS, Chattanooga, TN), Gaby Blum (Monument Mountain Regional HS, Great Barrington, MA), Charlie Camp (ARHS), Jim Carter (Saugus HS, Saugus, MA), Jack Czajkowski (Great Falls Middle School, Montague, MA), John Dark (Brainerd HS, Chattanooga, TN), Steve Degon (Central HS), Ed Eckel (Georgetown Day School, Washington, DC), Jen DuBois (NMH), Jake Foster (Hixson HS, Hixson, TN), Bill Fraser (Chattanooga Phoenix School 3, Chattanooga, TN), Ken Gano (Hixson HS), Dennis Gilbert (Taconic HS, Pittsfield, MA), Craig Hefner (NMH), Ray Janke (Chicopee HS, Chicopee, MA), Aaron Kropf (ARHS), Bernie Lally (Chicopee HS), Melany O'Connor (NMH), Michael

Oliphant (Millis HS, Millis, MA), Hughes Pack (NMH), Jerry Pate (Chattanooga School for Arts and Sciences, Chattanooga, TN), Kirk Rau (Tyner HS), Jessie Royal (Dade County HS, Trenton, GA), Cheryl Ryan (Hoosac Valley Regional HS, Adams, MA), John Safko (The University of South Carolina, Columbia, SC), Glenda Schmidt (Slidell HS, Slidell, LA), Lisa Schmitt (NMH), Steve Schultheis (Saugus HS), Lance Simpson (NMH), Mark Walcroft (Taconic HS), Mark Wenig (CSAS), Maxine Willis (Gettysburg HS, Gettysburg, PA), and Tom Winn (McMain HS, New Orleans, LA). They often had little warning about what and when materials would arrive, and usually had just a few days to prepare themselves to do the activities in class. We appreciate their patience and understanding. We also thank them for recommending that we create extensive teacher support materials. Although this addition has nearly doubled the scope of the project, it is a welcome change, and every teacher who uses the Minds•On Physics materials is indebted to them.

We thank Kris Chapman and Maggie Coffin for many of the drawings used in the activities. They brought a style and grace to the figures that none of us could ever match. We thank Ian Beatty for creating the Town of King's Court. We also thank Gary Bradway (Berkshire Community College, Pittsfield, MA), for his frequent help with conceptualizing and revising the early activities; Jerry Touger (Curry College, Milton, MA), for his help writing the Reader; and George Collison (The Concord Consortium, Concord, MA), for showing us how hands-on activities may be combined with minds-on activities.

Thanks to Allan Feldman (University of Massachusetts, Amherst, MA) and the rest of his evaluation team (Karla, Jim, Ed, Sonal, and Aaron) for evaluating the materials and its implementation.

We are thankful to Kendall/Hunt for publishing these materials. We are particularly thankful to the people at K/H for their many ideas and suggestions, especially regarding the format and style of these materials.

Special thanks also to all our friends and relatives.

Bill Leonard
Bob Dufresne
Bill Gerace
Jose Mestre

The UMass Physics Education Research Group
Department of Physics & Astronomy
Box 34525
University of Massachusetts
Amherst, MA 01003-4525 USA

Visit us on the Web at http://umperg.physics.umass.edu/

Activities

cs·1–31:
COMPLEX
SYSTEMS

CS·1

Exploring Ideas About Fluids

Purpose and Expected Outcome

In this activity, you will explore some phenomena involving fluids and record your ideas and impressions. Fluids appear to behave in very different ways than solid objects. Even more interesting is the manner in which solid objects and fluids interact with each other.

Prior Experience / Knowledge Needed

You need no formal knowledge of fluids. You should base your responses on your own ideas and experiences. You should know the basic concepts of *force*, *mass*, and *weight*, and you should know how to apply them to different situations.

Explanation of Activity

There are two parts in this activity. In the first part, you will record your ideas about fluids and compare them with your classmates. In the second part, you will build some of the arrangements described in part A, and test to see if your predictions are correct.

PART A: Recording Your Ideas About Fluids

For each of the following questions provide an answer and explain why you think your response is correct. Be prepared to share your ideas with your classmates.

A1. Oil is poured into a beaker containing some water. What happens to the oil? Explain.

A2. A tank containing water has a tap connected near the bottom. (See diagram at right.) A tube is attached to the tap so that there is no leakage. Assume that the tap in the diagram is turned on allowing water to flow from the tank.

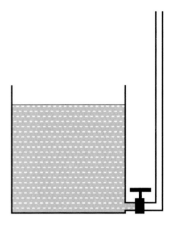

   (a) On a copy of this diagram, indicate the height to which you think the water will rise inside the tube. Explain your reasoning.

   (b) Is there any chance that the water will overflow the tube? Explain.

A3. A block of wood and a block of metal of equal weight are placed in a beaker containing water. What happens to each block? Explain.

A4. Each of the four situations below shows a different arrangement of a beaker of water, a wooden block, a metal block, and a platform scale. How do you think the readings on the four scales compare to each other? Put the four situations in order of their scale readings from least to greatest. Explain.

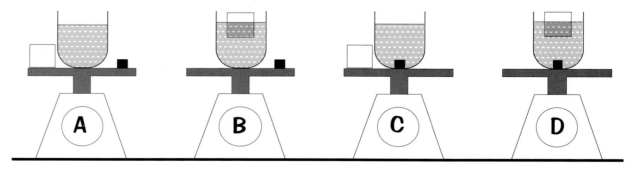

continued

A5. A large beaker of water sits on a scale. A wooden dowel (that would float if you let go of it) is inserted into the water until 10cm of it is submerged. Does the scale reading increase, decrease, or remain the same? Explain.

A6. A large beaker of water sits on a scale. A metal rod (that would sink if you let go of it) is inserted into the water until 10cm of it is submerged.

(a) Does the scale reading increase, decrease, or remain the same?

(b) If the reading changes, how does the change compare to the change occurring in question A5? (I.e., is the change larger than, smaller than, or the same as the change in A5?)

A7. Each of the four situations below shows a different arrangement. The beakers in A and C contain water, while the beakers in B and D contain oil. Initially all four beakers of fluid weigh the same. Identical metal rods are inserted into the beakers. In beakers A and B, the rod is inserted until 10cm of it is submerged. In beakers C and D, the rod rests on the bottom and side of the beaker and is completely submerged in fluid. How do the scale readings compare to each other? Put the four situations in order of their scale readings from least to greatest. Explain.

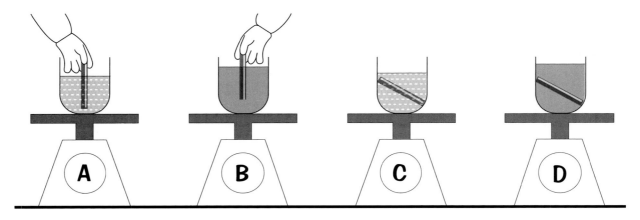

PART B: Verifying Your Predictions

To do this part of the activity you will need the following materials:

- two beakers;
- water;
- oil;
- a long tube of transparent plastic;
- a funnel that fits snugly into the plastic tube;
- one platform scale;
- one block of wood;
- one block of metal;
- one metal rod; and
- one wooden dowel.

In each of the situations below record your observations and state whether what you observe agrees with your predictions (from part A). In each case, state whether you still think your reasoning is correct, and if necessary, describe any changes in your reasoning.

B1. Pour some oil into a beaker partially filled with water.

(a) Describe in detail what happens.

(b) Does this agree with your description in A1? Explain why or why not. Describe any changes in your reasoning.

B2. Attach your funnel to one end of your tube. Have a classmate hold the other end of the tube at the height of the funnel as shown. Slowly pour water into the funnel. Keep filling until the funnel is half full of water.

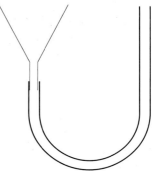

(a) Describe what happens. In particular, compare the level of the water in the free end of the tube to the level of the water in the funnel. Which is higher?

(b) Does this result surprise you? Explain. Does this result agree with your prediction in A2? Why or why not? Describe any changes in your reasoning about this situation.

B3. Now remove some of the water in the tube until its level is well below the funnel (see representation to the right). Pour some oil into the funnel.

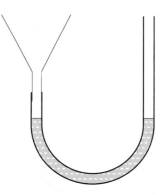

(a) Compare the heights of the liquids in the two sides of the tube. Is the height of the top of the oil higher or lower than the top of the water?

(b) Does this result surprise you? Explain why or why not.

continued

B4. Using a floating wooden block and a metal block, construct the situations shown in A4.

(a) Record the scale reading for each arrangement. Which is the smallest? the largest?

(b) Do your observations agree with what you predicted in part A? Why or why not? Describe any changes in your reasoning about these situations.

B5. Place a beaker partially filled with water on a scale. Lower a wooden dowel slowly into the water.

(a) Does the scale reading increase, decrease, or remain the same?

(b) Does your observation agree with what you predicted in A5? Explain. Describe any changes in your reasoning about this situation.

B6. Place a beaker partially filled with water on a scale. Lower a metal rod slowly into the water.

(a) Does the scale reading increase, decrease, or remain the same?

(b) Does your observation agree with what you predicted in A6(a)? Explain. Describe any changes in your reasoning about this situation.

(c) How does the final scale reading compare with the final scale reading in B5 above?

(d) Does this result agree with what you predicted in A6(b)? Describe any changes in your reasoning about this situation.

B7. Using a metal rod, a beaker, some water, and some oil, construct the four situations shown in A7. (Make sure the weights of oil and water are identical to each other.)

(a) Record the scale reading for each arrangement. Which is smallest? Which is largest?

(b) Do your observations agree with what you predicted in part A? Why or why not? Describe any changes in your reasoning about these situations.

Reflection

R1. If an object floats when put into water, will it float when put into all other liquids? Explain. If not, describe a situation in which something floats in water but sinks in another fluid.

R2. Are your explanations in B1 and B3 consistent with each other? In particular, imagine a horizontal line drawn where the oil and water meet. Compare the oil on the left to the water above the line on the right. What quantities are different? What quantities are the same?

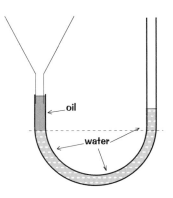

R3. Re-consider situation B3. What would happen if instead of oil, you poured into the funnel a fluid that sank in water?

R4. How would you define a *fluid*? What properties must a substance have to qualify as a fluid? Does air qualify as a fluid? Do you know anything that will float on air?

R5. Are your results in B4 and B7 consistent with each other? Explain why or why not.

CS·2

More Exploring Ideas About Fluids

Purpose and Expected Outcome

In this hands-on activity you will explore your ideas about weighing solids, fluids, and substances dissolved in fluid. You will find that there are many similarities between these three seemingly different scenarios.

Prior Experience / Knowledge Needed

You need no formal knowledge of fluids, chemistry, mixing, or dissolving. As in CS·1 (*Exploring Ideas About Fluids*), you should base all responses on your own ideas and experiences. You should know the concepts of *force*, *mass*, and *weight*, and you should be able to apply them to different situations.

Equipment / Materials Needed

To do this activity you will need the following materials (or their equivalents):

- one platform scale, capable of measuring to the nearest 1 gram or better
- a block of wood, small enough to fit in the beaker, but at least 5cm on a side
- water

- one beaker, capable of holding at least 500mL ($1mL = 1cm^3$; $500cm^3 = 1/2\,L$)
- a piece of metal, smaller than the block of wood, but at least 3cm on a side
- salt, at least 200g

Explanation of Activity

There are three situations to consider in this activity. In the first, you will weigh two solid objects in different configurations. In the second, you will weigh solids and fluids in different configurations. In the third, you will dissolve salt into water and do some more measurements.

SITUATION A: Weighing Solid Objects

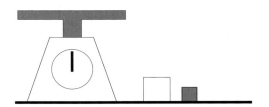

A1. Place the wooden block on the scale.

    (a) Draw this situation.

    (b) What is the scale reading?

    (c) What does the scale reading represent?

A2. Now place the metal block on the scale instead.

    (a) Draw this situation.

    (b) What is the scale reading?

    (c) What does the scale reading represent?

A3. Now place the blocks on the scale side-by-side.

    (a) Draw this situation.

    (b) What do you <u>expect</u> the scale reading to be? Explain.

    (c) What is the scale reading?

    (d) What does the scale reading represent?

A4. Now place the blocks on the scale with the metal one on top of the wooden one.

    (a) Draw this situation.

    (b) What do you <u>expect</u> the scale reading to be? Explain.

    (c) What is the scale reading?

    (d) What does the scale reading represent?

SITUATION B: Weighing Solids and Fluids Interacting With Each Other

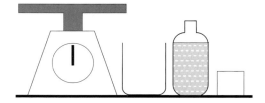

B1. Weigh the beaker.

    (a) Draw this situation.

    (b) What is the scale reading?

    (c) What is the weight of the beaker?

B2. Now weigh the beaker half filled with water.

    (a) Draw this situation.

    (b) What is the scale reading?

    (c) What is the weight of the water? Explain.

continued

B3. Weigh the block, with it next to the beaker half filled with water.

    (a) Draw this situation.

    (b) What do you <u>expect</u> the scale reading to be? Explain.

    (c) What is the scale reading?

    (d) What is the weight of the block?

B4. Weigh the block, this time with it floating in the water.

    (a) Draw this situation.

    (b) What do you <u>expect</u> the scale reading to be? Explain.

    (c) What is the scale reading?

    (d) What is the weight of the block?

SITUATION C: Weighing a Substance Dissolved in a Fluid

C1. Remove the block from part B, and re-weigh the beaker half filled with water.

    (a) What is the scale reading?

    (b) Is this what you expected? Explain any deviations from your answer to B2(b).

C2. Measure out 200g of salt.

    (a) Draw this situation.

    (b) What is the scale reading?

    (c) What does the scale reading represent?

    (d) How do you know you have 200g of salt?

C3. Dissolve the 200g of salt (from C2) into the water.

    (a) Draw this situation.

    (b) What do you <u>expect</u> the scale reading to be? Explain.

    (c) What is the scale reading?

    (d) What does the scale reading represent?

Reflection

R1. Compare situations A and B. How are they similar? different?

R2. Consider configuration A3. Of the four configurations in situation B, which is most like configuration A3? Explain.

R3. Consider configuration B4. Which configuration in situation A is most like configuration B4? Explain.

R4. Consider configuration C2. Which configurations in situations A and B are most like configuration C2? Explain.

R5. Which scale readings were unexpected to you? What did you learn as a result? How has your understanding changed during this activity?

Investigating Pressure and Density

Purpose and Expected Outcome

In this activity you will explore the ideas of *pressure* and *density*. These concepts are very important when studying fluids. You may feel that you already understand the concept of *density*, having encountered it before. Unfortunately, many times we fail to distinguish between *density* and *mass*, and this failure becomes a source of confusion when considering fluids. While the concept of *pressure* is related to *force*, it is also quite different, and it is important to distinguish between these two ideas. After completing the activity you should be sensitive to the distinction between *mass* and *density* and also be aware of the difference between *force* and *pressure*.

Prior Experience / Knowledge Needed

You should know the concepts of *force*, *mass*, and *weight*, and you should be able to apply them to different situations. You should be able to draw free body diagrams and use them to analyze a physical situation. You should be able to apply Newton's 2nd law to different situations. You should have some experience with the concepts of *pressure* and *density*.

The *density* of a substance is a measure of the amount of mass contained in a standard volume of that substance. The symbol used for density is the Greek letter ρ (*rho*, which is pronounced "row"), and its MKS units are kg/m^3.

The *average density* of an object made of several substances is the ratio of its total mass divided by its total volume:

$$\rho_{ave} \equiv \frac{M_{total}}{V_{total}} \qquad \text{definition of average density}$$

A *uniform* object contains the same substance throughout its volume, so the density is the same everywhere throughout its volume as well, and is equal to the average density for the object. When an object is not uniform, we can estimate the density at each point of the object by considering only a very small volume of material and finding the ratio of mass divided by volume.

Pressure is the measure of the strength of the normal force exerted on a standard, flat area of a surface. The symbol for pressure is P, and its MKS unit is the Pascal (Pa), where 1Pa = 1N/m^2. Pressure is defined at every point in a fluid. Pressure has no direction associated with it, so it is a scalar quantity. Given a small, flat area A completely immersed in a fluid, the magnitude of the normal force exerted by the fluid on this area is PA. (We assume that the area is so small that the pressure does not vary over the surface.) The direction of this force is perpendicular to the plane that contains the area. In other words, the force exerted by the fluid is *normal* to the surface, and like the normal force, always pushes. Thus, the direction of the force, a vector quantity, depends upon the orientation of the surface being considered. So, for instance, the force that air exerts on a wall is horizontal, the force air exerts on the ceiling or the underside of a table is directed upward, and the force that water exerts on the bottom of a glass is down.

Explanation of Activity

There are two parts in this activity. In the first part, you will explore the idea of *density* and how it applies in different situations. In the second part, you will explore the idea of *pressure*.

PART A: Comparing Mass and Density

A1. Consider the following items: a coin, a basketball, a bicycle, a ping-pong ball, a small bag of water (no air!), and a baseball. Make a list of these items in order of increasing (a) mass, (b) volume, and (c) average density.

A2. Consider the situation shown below, in which two fluids, X and Y, are mixed together.

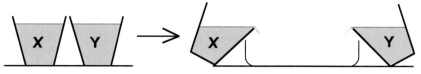

On a copy of the table below, fill in the missing information.

	Fluid X				Fluid Y				Mixture of X and Y		
	fluid	m (g)	V (cm^3)	ρ (g/cm^3)	fluid	m (g)	V (cm^3)	ρ (g/cm^3)		m (g)	V (cm^3)	ρ (g/cm^3)
(a)	milk		20	1.03	milk		20				
(b)	milk				milk		10			30	
(c)	oil	18	20		water		20				
(d)	oil	20			water	20					
(e)	syrup		20		syrup	10					1.3

A3. Consider the six objects described below. Put them in order from smallest to largest by (a) mass, and by (b) average density.

   P. A sponge ball (or Nerf® ball) having diameter D.

   Q. A basketball, diameter D, filled with air.

   R. A basketball, diameter D, fully deflated (no air).

   S. A basketball, diameter D, filled with helium.

   T. A hollow, metallic ball. Its diameter is D; the thickness of the metal is the same as the thickness of rubber used to make a basketball; and the ball has no air in it.

   U. A hollow, metallic ball (as in situation T above) filled with helium.

A4. Compare the average densities of four amounts of water under the circumstances described below. Put them in order from smallest to largest average density.

   W. one cubic meter of steam.

   X. 18 grams of ice.

   Y. 12 cubic centimeters of water at the bottom of a bottle of oil.

   Z. 19 cubic centimeters of water on the surface of the Moon.

PART B: Comparing Force and Pressure

Sometimes the important physical quantity in a situation is the force, while at other times the important quantity is the pressure. Recognizing which is the relevant quantity requires having a good understanding of the difference between force and pressure.

Below are descriptions of some common situations. In each case you are asked to consider two variations of the situation and to specify which variation produces (a) the larger force and (b) the larger pressure. Finally, in (c) you will answer a question about the situation and indicate which feature, the force or the pressure, is more relevant for answering it.

B1. Two women have the same weight. Woman A is sitting on a wide cement step, while woman B is sitting on a narrow metal railing.

    (a) Which woman has a larger normal force exerted on her?

    (b) Which woman has a larger pressure exerted on her due to what she is sitting on?

    (c) Which woman is more comfortable? Why? Which quantity, force or pressure, is more relevant for answering this question?

B2. Two karate students are trying to break a board. Student A hits the board with his open palm, while student B uses the side of his hand instead. Both students deliver the same impulse for the same time interval.

    (a) Which student exerts a larger average force on the board?

    (b) Which student exerts a larger average pressure on the board?

    (c) Which board is more likely to break? Why? Which quantity, force or pressure, is more relevant for answering this question?

B3. Two identical scales are each used to weigh two identical blocks. On scale A, the blocks are side-by-side on the platform, while on scale B, the two blocks are stacked.

    (a) Which platform has a larger normal force exerted on it?

    (b) Which platform has a larger pressure exerted on it due to the blocks?

    (c) Which scale reads a larger value? Why? Which quantity, force or pressure, is more relevant for answering this question?

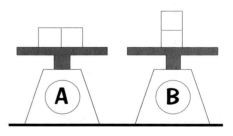

B4. Two identical balloons are inflated with air. Balloon A has less air inside of it than balloon B.

    (a) Which balloon has a larger weight?

    (b) Which balloon has a larger pressure inside of it?

    (c) Which balloon is larger? Why? Which quantity, force or pressure, is more relevant for answering this question?

B5. Two identical balloons are inflated until they are the same size. Balloon A is filled with air, while balloon B is filled with helium instead.

    (a) Which balloon has a larger weight?

    (b) Which balloon has a larger pressure inside of it?

    (c) Which balloon has more gas inside it? Why? Which quantity, force or pressure, is more relevant for answering this question?

B6. Two men have about the same weight. Man A is walking across the snow using snow shoes, while man B is walking across the snow using sneakers.

    (a) Which man exerts a larger normal force on the snow?

    (b) Which man exerts a larger pressure on the snow?

    (c) Which man is more likely to sink into the snow? Why? Which quantity, force or pressure, is more relevant for answering this question?

Reflection

R1. In question A2, what conservation principles did you use to fill in the table? In other words, what physical quantities were the same before and after mixing the two fluids together?

R2. (a) Which is heavier, a fully inflated basketball or an uninflated basketball? Explain. Why does a fully inflated basketball float in water, while an uninflated one sinks in water?

(b) Which is heavier, a balloon filled with helium or an uninflated balloon? Explain. Why does a helium-filled balloon rise in air, while an uninflated one falls in air?

R3. Is the average density of a mixture always equal to the average of the densities of its components? Explain why or why not. If not, give an example of a situation in which the average density is not equal to the average of the individual densities. Under what conditions is the average density of a mixture equal to the average of the densities of its components?

R4. Under what conditions does a scale <u>not</u> measure the weight of an object?

R5. In part B, how many times did you confuse pressure with force? Are you confident that you understand the difference between pressure and force? What are the fundamental similarities between pressure and force? What are the fundamental differences? Under what conditions are the force and pressure the same?

Relating Pressure Ideas to Different Situations

Purpose and Expected Outcome

In this activity you will investigate how concepts developed to describe the behavior of rigid bodies can be used to describe *static* fluids (in other words, fluids that are not moving). In some cases it will be necessary to modify our concepts in order to be able to deal with the fluid's ability to assume any shape.

Just as with the ideas of *work* and *acceleration*, we must be careful not to confuse the formal idea of *pressure* with our everyday use of the term.

The purpose of this activity is to acquaint you with the fact that pressure can vary with position in a fluid.

Prior Experience / Knowledge Needed

You should know the concepts of *force*, *mass*, and *weight*, and you should know how to apply them in different situations. You should be able to use free-body diagrams to analyze a physical situation. You should be able to solve Newton's 2nd law problems.

Explanation of Activity

There are two parts in this activity.

PART A: Comparing Fluids and Solids

Consider a block and a beaker of water sitting at rest on a table as shown. The block and the water each has a mass M and a bottom surface area A.

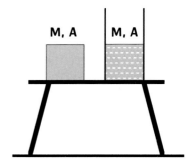

Answer the questions below, which compare the forces and pressures on the block with the forces and pressures on the water.

A1. (a) Draw a free-body diagram for the block, clearly labeling each force.

(b) Draw a free-body diagram for the <u>water</u> in the beaker, clearly labeling each force.

A2. (a) What is the total force exerted by the table on the bottom of the block?

(b) What is the total force exerted by the beaker on the bottom of the water?

A3. (a) What is the average force per unit area exerted by the table on the bottom of the block?

(b) What is the average force per unit area exerted by the beaker on the bottom of the water?

A second identical block is now placed on top of the original block.

The amount of water in the beaker is now doubled.

A4. (a) What is the force exerted by the table on the blocks?

(b) What is the force exerted by the beaker on the water?

A5. (a) What is the average force per unit area (pressure) exerted by the table on the blocks?

(b) What is the average force per unit area (pressure) exerted by the beaker on the bottom of the water?

The top block is now moved to be beside the original block.

The water is now poured into a beaker having twice the bottom surface area of the original.

A6. (a) What is the total force exerted by the table on the blocks?

(b) What is the total force exerted by the beaker on the water?

A7. (a) What is the pressure exerted by the table on the blocks?

(b) What is the pressure exerted by the beaker on the bottom of the water?

PART B: Finding Change in Pressure with Depth

In this part, we continue to use an analogy with a mechanical system. Now we use it to determine the pressure in a fluid as a function of depth.

A block of density ρ, cross-sectional area A, and height h sits on top of an identical block as shown.

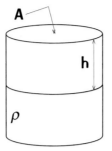

A fluid of density ρ fills a glass beaker of cross-sectional area A as shown.

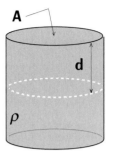

B1. (a) What is the mass of the upper block?

(b) What are the magnitudes of the forces that the two blocks exert on each other?

(c) What is the average pressure that each block exerts on the other?

(d) In analogy with the two-block system, determine the pressure in the fluid at depth d below the surface of the fluid.

Now imagine that a force **F** is applied to the top of the block as shown.

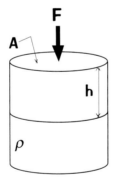

For the fluid, imagine that there is a pressure P_0 (for instance, air pressure) exerted on the top of the fluid.

B2. (a) What is the average pressure P_0 exerted on the top face of the top block?

(b) What is the force that each block exerts on the other?

(c) What is the pressure that each block exerts on the other? (Leave your answer in terms of h, ρ, A, P_0 and any other universal constants you need.)

(d) In analogy with the two-block system, determine the pressure in the fluid at depth d below the surface of the fluid. (Leave your answer in terms of d, ρ, A, P_0 and any other universal constants you need.)

Reflection

R1. In part A, are there any forces on the water's free-body diagram (A1, part (b)) that are not on the block's free-body diagram? Explain why or why not.

R2. In part A, when you drew the free-body diagram for the water, did you ignore any forces exerted by the glass beaker? How did you determine the direction of the force exerted by the glass beaker? Are there any other forces that you ignored?

R3. (a) Which of the following factors would you say <u>directly</u> affect the pressure at a certain point inside a fluid?

- ❏ size of the beaker
- ❏ mass of the fluid
- ❏ volume of the fluid
- ❏ kind of fluid (water, oil, syrup, etc.)
- ❏ state of the fluid (gas, liquid, solid, etc.)
- ❏ rigidity (or flexibility) of the beaker (e.g., glass vs. plastic)
- ❏ how far the point is located from the bottom of the beaker
- ❏ how far the point is located from the surface of the fluid
- ❏ how far the point is located from the side of the beaker
- ❏ how far the point is located from the top of the beaker
- ❏ where the beaker is located

(b) For each factor you have chosen, give an example of how the pressure would be affected, and explain the effect it has on the pressure.

(c) Are there any other factors that might affect the pressure inside a fluid?

R4. Is it possible to find the pressure at a certain height h above the <u>bottom</u> of a container filled with fluid? If so, how? If not, why not? What additional information is needed to find the pressure?

R5. (a) List the features that air and water have in common.

(b) In what ways are air and water different?

(c) Do you think that air qualifies as a *fluid*? Explain why or why not.

Exploring Interactions Between Static Fluids and Rigid Bodies

Purpose and Expected Outcome

In this activity you will investigate how concepts developed to describe the motion of rigid objects can be used to describe static fluids and their interactions with rigid objects. In some cases it will be necessary to use new concepts (such as *pressure*) in order to help deal with a fluid's ability to spread out and conform to the shape of the container it is in. Other new concepts, such as *buoyancy*, will also be developed.

What you will find is that principles associated with static fluids are more easily represented and applied in terms of pressure and density. However, Newton's laws remain useful for explaining and understanding these new principles.

Prior Experience / Knowledge Needed

You should be familiar with the concepts of *force*, *mass*, and *weight*, and know how to apply them in a variety of different situations. You should be able to use free-body diagrams to analyze a physical situation. You should be able to solve Newton's 2nd law problems. You should also know how pressure varies with depth in a static fluid (that is, $P = P_0 + \rho g d$, where ρ is the density of the fluid, d is the depth below the surface, and P_0 is the pressure at the surface).

Explanation of Activity

There are three parts in this activity.

PART A: Analyzing Forces on a Body in a Static Fluid

Answer the questions below using your knowledge of forces and how to apply Newton's laws.

A1. Imagine a small cube-shaped sample of fluid located in the middle of a beaker of fluid as shown to the right.

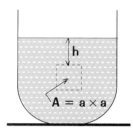

    (a) Identify the forces exerted on the cube of fluid. How many forces are exerted on the sample? Where are they located?

    (b) What is the net force on the sample? Explain.

    (c) Draw a free-body diagram for the cube of fluid. Which force do you think is the largest? Which is the smallest? Explain.

    (d) Compare the pressure on the top of the sample to the pressure on the bottom. Which is larger, or are they the same? Explain.

    (e) Compare the pressures on the vertical surfaces (left, right, front, and back) to each other. Which is the largest? Which is the smallest? Explain.

    (f) Is there a resultant force due to the pressures on all surfaces of the sample? If not, explain why not. If so, write an expression for its magnitude and direction.

A2. Consider a block of metal having the same dimensions and location as the sample of fluid above. The metal block is held in place using a piece of string suspended from the ceiling.

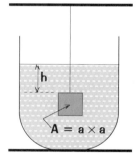

    (a) How does the pressure on any particular surface of the block compare to the pressure on the corresponding surface of the sample above?

    (b) How does the strength and direction of the force due to pressure from the surrounding fluid compare to the corresponding force on the sample above? Explain.

    (c) Explain using forces why the metal block would sink when the piece of string is cut.

    (d) Explain using forces why a cube of STYROFOAM placed in the same location in the fluid would rise when released.

Summary of Part A

You have derived an expression for the *buoyant force*, and you now know that its source is the pressure in a fluid, which increases with depth. Later, you will learn a more general expression that applies in every situation.

PART B: Comparing Forces on a Body in a Static Fluid

This is a hands-on activity. You will need a small plastic container that can seal very tightly (and not let any fluid into or out of it). The container must be transparent enough to allow you to see the level of the fluid inside it. Also, you will need some water, some syrup, and a beaker large enough to fit the container.

B1. Fill the plastic container with water and seal it.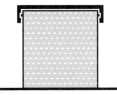
- (a) Predict what you think will happen when the full container is put into a large beaker of water.
- (b) Put the full container into the water and describe what happens. How does this compare to your prediction in (a)?
- (c) Explain why the full container behaves this way.

B2. Fill one-fourth of the plastic container with water and seal it.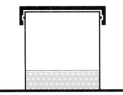
- (a) Predict what you think will happen when the container is put into a beaker of water. In particular, draw how you think the situation will look. Be sure to indicate the level of the water inside the container.
- (b) Put the container into the water and describe what happens. How does this compare to your prediction in (a)?
- (c) Explain why the container behaves this way.

B3. Fill one-half of the plastic container with water and seal it. Repeat parts (a), (b) and (c) in B2 above.

B4. Fill three-fourths of the plastic container with water and seal it. Repeat parts (a), (b) and (c) in B2 above.

B5. Fill the plastic container with syrup and seal it.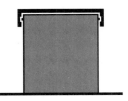
- (a) Predict what you think will happen when the full container is put into a beaker of water.
- (b) Put the full container into the water and describe what happens. How does this compare to your prediction in (a)?
- (c) Explain why the full container behaves this way.

B6. Compare the forces due to water pressure on the outsides of containers B1 through B5. Put them in order from largest to smallest net force due to water pressure. Explain your answer.

PART C: Measuring and Comparing Forces on a Body in a Static Fluid

The beginning of this part is to be done hands-on. You will need a small container that seals tightly (without letting any water into it) and a large beaker. Also you will need some small dense materials that you can add to the container to change its mass, such as coins, sand, or BBs. Finally you will need a method for weighing the container and its contents, both when it is in the water and when it is out of the water. For instance, you can attach a loop of string to the lid of your container using duct tape, and then weigh the container using a spring scale.

After completing the hands-on portion (C1–C3), answer the follow-up questions using your knowledge of forces and how to apply Newton's laws. Be sure to keep the water level in the beaker at least twice as high as the height of the container.

C1. Put coins into the container until it <u>just</u> sinks with the lid on.

(a) Weigh the container (and its contents) out of the water.

(b) Weigh the container submerged in the water.

(c) Compute the difference in the weights.

C2. Now <u>double</u> (roughly) the number of coins in the container.

(a) Weigh the container (and its contents) out of the water.

(b) Weigh the container in the water, with the top of the container near (but below) the surface of the water.

(c) Compute the difference in the weights.

(d) Does the weight of the container change as you lower it even further into the water?

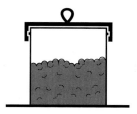

C3. Now <u>fill</u> the container with coins.

(a) Weigh the container (and its contents) out of the water.

(b) Weigh the container in the water, with the top of the container near (but below) the surface of the water.

(c) Compute the difference in the weights.

(d) Does the weight of the container change as you lower it even further into the water?

C4. (a) How do the differences in weights (in and out of the water) compare to each other?

(b) What does the difference in weights represent in each case?

(c) Explain why the differences are all about the same. What else is the same in each case?

Reflection

R1. In part B, how many of your predictions were correct? Why do you suppose some were incorrect? What feature or idea do you think caused your incorrect prediction? What have you learned as a result of doing part B?

R2. (a) In part C, did you really measure the weight of the container (and its contents) when it was in the water, or did you measure something else? What did you really measure?

    (b) What must be true about a situation for the scale reading to be equal to the weight of the object?

R3. Reconsider situations C2 and C3, in which the containers sink when put in water.

    (a) How did the force due to pressure on the bottom of the container change as you lowered the container deeper into the water (<u>after</u> it was fully submerged)? In other words, did the pressure get larger, smaller, or stay the same?

    (b) How did the measured "weight" of the container change as you lowered the fully submerged container deeper into the water?

    (c) Are these two effects consistent with each other? In other words, how is it possible that one could change while the other remains about the same? Explain.

R4. Reconsider situation B4, in which ³/₄ of the container is filled with water.

    (a) Imagine putting the container into a beaker of oil instead of water. What do you think will happen? Where will the water line (inside the container) be compared to the surface of the oil? Explain.

    (b) Imagine putting the container into a beaker of syrup instead of water or oil. What will happen? Where will the water line (inside the container) be compared to the surface of the syrup? Explain.

Comparing Interactions Between Static Fluids and Rigid Bodies

Purpose and Expected Outcome

This activity is a continuation of the previous activity. You will investigate more deeply how concepts such as *volume*, *mass*, *density*, *pressure*, and *force* can be used to understand fluids by comparing similar situations.

Prior Experience / Knowledge Needed

You should know how to apply the concepts of *force*, *mass*, and *weight* to any situation. You should be familiar with the concepts of *volume*, *density*, and *pressure*. You should know why the pressure in a fluid increases with increasing depth.

Explanation of Activity

There are two parts in this activity. In the first part, you will compare situations in which objects are completely submerged in a fluid. In the second part, you will compare situations in which objects are floating.

PART A: Comparing Objects Submerged in a Static Fluid

In all six situations below, the bottom area of the object is the same. Object A is a block of metal, which sinks to the bottom of the water. Object B is a tall plastic container, which is filled with water. <u>Just</u> enough coins are added so that the container sinks to the bottom. Object C is an identical container in which there is no water, but <u>just</u> enough coins are added so that the container (again) sinks to the bottom. Object D is identical to C, except that the number of coins is doubled. Object E is a shorter plastic container (than B, C, or D) filled with water. Just enough coins are added so that the sealed container sinks to the bottom. Object F is identical to E, except that it is put into the water on top of metal block A. (The block is separate; it is not part of object F.)

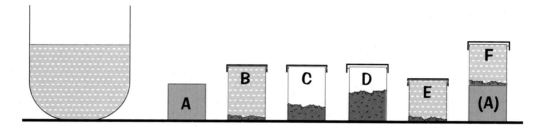

A1. On a separate sheet of paper, draw situations A through F, showing each object completely submerged in a beaker of water.

A2. (a) Which object (A–F) has the largest <u>volume</u> submerged? the smallest? Explain.

(b) How do the volumes submerged compare to each other? (Put them in order from largest to smallest.)

A3. (a) Which object <u>displaces</u> the largest volume of water? the smallest? Explain.

(b) How do the volumes displaced compare to each other? (Put them in order from largest to smallest.)

A4. (a) In which situation is the <u>water level</u> is the highest? the lowest? Explain.

(b) How do the water levels compare to each other? (Put them in order from highest to lowest.)

A5. (a) Which object has the largest <u>force</u> exerted on it by the water? the smallest? Explain.

(b) How do the forces compare to each other? (Put them in order from largest to smallest.)

A6. (a) Which object has the largest <u>weight</u>? the smallest? Explain.

(b) How do the weights compare to each other? (Put them in order.)

PART B: Comparing Objects Floating in a Static Fluid

In the first four situations below, the bottom area of the object is the same. Object A is a block of wood, which floats with its bottom a distance d below the surface of the water. Object B is a tall plastic container, which is filled with water until it floats with its bottom also a distance d below the surface of the water. Object C is identical to B, except that coins are added until it also floats with its bottom a distance d below the surface of the water. Object D is a shorter plastic container (than B or C) filled with water until it floats with its bottom a distance d below the surface. Object E is a set of small wooden blocks which cause the level of the water to be the same as in situation A.

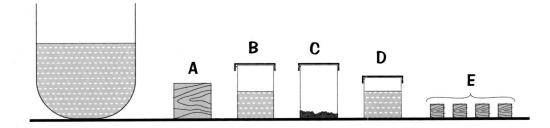

B1. On a separate sheet of paper, draw situations A through E, showing each object floating in a beaker of water.

B2. (a) Which object has the largest <u>fraction</u> of its volume submerged? Explain.
　　　(b) Which has the smallest fraction submerged? Explain.

B3. (a) Which object has the largest <u>volume</u> submerged? Explain.
　　　(b) Which has the smallest volume submerged? Explain.

B4. (a) Which object <u>displaces</u> the largest volume of water? Explain.
　　　(b) Which displaces the smallest volume of water? Explain.

B5. (a) Which <u>water level</u> is the highest? Explain.
　　　(b) Which water level is the lowest? Explain.

B6. (a) Which object has the largest <u>force</u> exerted on it by the water? Explain.
　　　(b) Which has the smallest force exerted on it by the water? Explain.

B7. (a) Which object has the largest <u>weight</u>? Explain.
　　　(b) Which has the smallest weight? Explain.

Integration of Ideas

This part of the activity is a challenge, in which your team will compete with other teams in trying to cause an object to have (what is called) *neutral buoyancy*. This means that the object neither floats nor sinks when put into a fluid. We will use water.

Your team will be given a plastic bath toy, which floats when filled with air, but sinks when completely filled with sand. The goal of this challenge is to put enough sand into the bath toy so that it (a) sinks when put into water, but also (b) has the smallest possible "weight" when hung from a spring scale with the toy completely submerged.

There are a few guidelines your group must follow during this challenge:

1. You cannot use trial and error to determine how much sand to put into the toy. Rather, you must use a strategic approach based on the ideas you have learned so far. Each team will be given exactly two attempts, <u>each with a different bath toy</u>.

2. The bath toy must sink when put into water. (This is necessary so that there is a non-zero scale reading.)

3. The bath toy with the smallest scale reading when "weighed" in water wins the competition. The toy must be completely submerged during the weighing.

4. If two or more teams have the same smallest scale reading, then the team with the heaviest object will win. In other words, if the bath toy is "weighed" in water and out of water, the smallest ratio of these two scale readings wins.

Reflection

R1. In A5, what is the direction of the force exerted by the water? Explain.

R2. (a) Describe at least two methods for determining the total volume of something. Could oil be used to measure the total volume? Explain. Could air be used to measure the total volume? Explain. What if the object floats in water? Could you still determine its total volume? How?

     (b) For a floating object, describe a method for determining the volume that is below the surface of the fluid.

R3. Which of the following features <u>directly</u> affects the buoyant force on an object when put into a fluid in a beaker?

❏ size of the beaker	❏ mass of the object	❏ volume displaced by object
❏ mass of the fluid	❏ volume of the object	❏ where the beaker is located
❏ volume of the fluid	❏ density of the object	❏ kind of fluid (oil, water, etc.)

Reasoning About Static Fluids

Purpose and Expected Outcome

In previous activities on fluids, you used new concepts (for example, *pressure* and *density*) along with old concepts and principles (*force*, *mass*, Newton's 2nd law) to analyze static fluids. In the process you developed some special principles for <u>static</u> fluids (a relationship between *pressure* and *depth*, a relationship between the buoyant force and the weight of the displaced fluid). In this activity you will use what you have learned from previous activities to reason about fluid situations and to solve problems involving static fluids. This activity will require that you apply your knowledge to a variety of new situations.

Prior Experience / Knowledge Needed

You should know the concepts of *mass*, *force*, and *weight*, and be able to use them to analyze, reason, and solve problems. You should be able to identify the forces exerted on an object, including forces exerted by fluids, and be able to draw a free-body diagram for objects interacting with fluids. You should know how to solve Newton's 2nd law problems. You should know how the pressure in a fluid changes with depth in a static fluid (i.e., $P = P_0 + \rho g d$, where P_0 is the pressure at the surface of the fluid, ρ is the density of the fluid, and d is the depth of a particular point of interest in the fluid). Finally, you should be familiar with the idea that the total force exerted by a fluid (the buoyant force) is equal to the weight of the displaced fluid.

Explanation of Activity

Reason about the following situations using your knowledge of *force*, *mass*, *acceleration*, and Newton's 2nd law. In your explanations, use as many new ideas as possible, such as *pressure*, *density*, and *volume displaced*. Wherever possible, verify your conclusion using real objects (i.e., hands-on).

A1. Consider two containers. They have the same cross-sectional areas on the bottom, but one has sloped sides, while the other has vertical sides. (See diagram.) The containers are placed empty on platform scales, which are adjusted to read zero. This means that when fluid is put into the containers, the scale reading is only the weight of the <u>fluid</u>. The containers are partially filled with water until they both have the same depth.

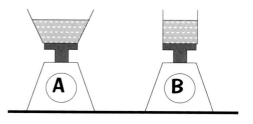

Consider the following argument:

   i. The densities of the fluids in the two containers are the same.

   ii. The fluid heights are the same.

   iii. The pressures on the bottoms of the containers are the same.

   iv. The areas of the bottoms of the containers are the same.

   v. The normal forces exerted by the fluids on the bottoms of the containers are the same.

   vi. The normal forces exerted by the containers on the fluids are the same.

   vii. Each normal force is equal to the weight of the fluid.

   viii. Therefore, the weights of the two samples of fluid are the same.

(a) Is the conclusion (statement *viii*) true or false? Explain why you think so.

(b) If the conclusion is true, explain how the container with more fluid can have the same weight as the container with less fluid.

(c) If the conclusion is false, identify the statement(s) above that is(are) invalid.

A2. Which weighs the most, a balloon filled with air, a balloon filled with helium, or an empty balloon? Explain. Which weighs the least? Explain.

A3. Consider the following claim: "A balloon filled with helium will rise to a certain height and stop, yet a rock will always sink to the bottom of a tank filled with water, no matter how deep the tank is." Is this claim reasonable? If so, explain why. If not, why not?

continued

A4. A glass is placed on a platform scale.

    (a) Is there any air between the glass and the upper surface of the scale? Explain.

    (b) Is there any air pressure exerting a force up on the bottom of the glass? Explain.

    (c) Is the scale reading <u>exactly</u> equal to the weight of the glass? If not, is the reading higher or lower than the weight? How much higher or lower? Explain.

A5. Two suction cups of similar design and material, but different sizes, are pressed securely onto a glass tabletop. Which suction cup would be harder to slide across the tabletop, or would they be about the same? Explain in detail.

A6. Each of the containers shown below consists of two tubes connected at the bottom so that fluid can flow between them. On a separate sheet of paper, draw the equilibrium situation that results in each case when fluid is added.

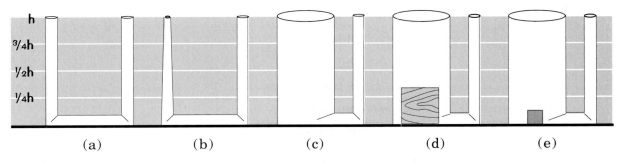

    (a) Water is poured into the left side until the surface on the left is located at $^1/_2h$. Then oil is poured into the right side until its upper surface is located at $^3/_4h$.

    (b) This is the same as (a), except that the left tube narrows uniformly as shown.

    (c) Water is poured into the left side until the right surface is located at $^1/_2h$.

    (d) This is the same as (c), except that a block of wood is inside the container when the water is poured in.

    (e) This is the same as (c), except that a block of metal is inside the container when the water is poured in.

A7. An ice cube is floating in a beaker of water. Vegetable oil is poured into the beaker until the ice is completely submerged in oil. Will the ice cube sink deeper into the water, float higher in the water, or remain at the same height after the oil is poured in? Explain.

A8. A suction cup is pressed firmly to the top of a platform scale.

    (a) What is the direction of the force that the suction cup exerts on the scale?

    (b) Compare the magnitude of the force that the scale exerts on the suction cup with the weight of the suction cup.

    (c) Will the scale read the weight of the suction cup? Explain why or why not.

Reflection

R1. (a) Did you use free-body diagrams to help you analyze any of the situations in this activity? Which situations?

(b) In general, what made you decide to draw (or not draw) a free-body diagram?

(c) Pick a situation for which you had difficulty answering the question(s) <u>and</u> for which you did not draw a free-body diagram. Go back and re-do the question using a free-body diagram to help you analyze the situation.

R2. Situation A2 in Activity CS·1 (*Exploring Ideas About Fluids*) is very similar to situation A6(c) in this activity. Compare your answer before to your answer in this activity. Has it changed? Why? What have you learned?

R3. Does a platform scale always read the weight of the object on it? Describe three different types of situations in which the scale does <u>not</u> read the weight of the object, with an example of each type.

R4. (a) Estimate the buoyant force on a 10cm cube of wood in air. Compare this value to the precision of your platform scales.

(b) Is it reasonable to ignore the effect of buoyancy in air when measuring the weight of common objects? Give two examples of situations in which the buoyant force is important and cannot be ignored when weighing something in air.

(c) What is different about these situations compared to the ones in which we can ignore the buoyant force?

Exploring Ideas About Moving Fluids

Purpose and Expected Outcome

Previous activities focused on learning new ideas and applying old ideas to situations involving <u>static</u> fluids. In this activity, you will begin looking at moving fluids. You will record your own thoughts and predictions about moving fluids.

Prior Experience / Knowledge Needed

You need no formal knowledge of moving fluids. You should base your responses on your own ideas and experiences. You should have some experience with static fluids, and you should know how basic concepts such as *force*, *mass*, and *weight* apply to fluids. You should have a basic understanding of new concepts relevant to fluids, such as *pressure* and *density*, and you should know basic relationships, such as how the pressure in a static fluid changes with depth.

REPRESENTING FLUID FLOW

Moving fluids present many challenges. The first is how to represent its flow using a static, two-dimensional drawing. We will use dotted lines to show the paths of the fluid as it flows through tubes or pipes. We imagine that molecules of the fluid that are on the dotted line in one part of a tube or pipe stay on the same line as they move through the tube or pipe. Molecules between the dotted lines remain between the lines.

Shown to the right is an example of how fluid flows through a pipe that is wider on the right side than on the left. Note that there is no information in the diagram about which direction (left or right) the fluid flows, and also

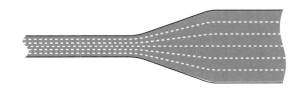

no information about how fast or slow the fluid is moving in different parts of the pipe.

Explanation of Activity

There are two parts in this activity. In the first part, you will record some observations about moving fluids and compare them with your classmates. In the second part, you will make some predictions based on your observations and then test to see if your predictions are correct.

PART A: Recording Your Observations About Moving Fluids

For each of the following situations (a) record your observations, (b) answer all associated questions, and (c) draw a diagram showing the motion of the fluid in the system. (This diagram should show the path of the molecules of fluid as in the diagram on the previous page.) Be prepared to share your ideas with your classmates.

A1. Suspend two sheets of paper as shown below. Use a hair dryer to blow air through the region between the two sheets of paper. (Blow the air parallel to the top edge of the paper.)

(a) Record what happens to the sheets of paper when the hair dryer is blowing.

(b) Is this what you expected? Explain.

(c) Make a diagram showing the positions of the two pieces of paper and the flow of air past them.

A2. Repeat situation A1 above with two ping-pong balls suspended approximately 2–3cm apart.

(a) Record what happens to the two ping-pong balls when the hair dryer is blowing.

(b) Is this what you expected? Explain.

(c) Make a diagram showing the positions of the ping-pong balls and the flow of air past them.

continued

A3. Place a ping-pong ball in a vertical stream of air flowing upwards from a hair dryer.

(a) Record what happens to the ping-pong ball.

(b) Is it possible to position the ping-pong ball so that it remains suspended at a fixed height above the hair dryer? Try it. What happens when you change the speed of the air blowing out of the hair dryer? Is it possible to tilt the hair dryer while keeping the ping-pong ball suspended in the stream of air? Try it. What is the largest angle you can tilt the hair dryer without losing the ball?

(c) Draw a diagram showing the position of the ping-pong ball suspended above the hair dryer and the flow of air past the ball.

A4. Fill a container (such as a large STYROFOAM or paper cup) with water. Place the container above something to catch the water as it pours out. Poke a hole in the side of the container near its bottom.

(a) Record what happens to the stream of water as the container empties.

(b) Does the water have a velocity just as it leaves the container? Explain why or why not? If so, does the velocity change as the level of water in the container changes? Explain why you think so. Describe the trajectory of the water after it leaves the container. How does the trajectory change as the container empties?

(c) Make a diagram showing the trajectory of the water and the flow of water both inside and outside the container.

A5. Make a *siphon* as shown to the right. The container of water should be large enough and the diameter of the tube should be small enough that the level of water does not change very quickly. (To start the flow of water, fill the tube with water and place a finger over each end. Put one end into the water and hold the other end lower than the end in the water. Remove your fingers. When the flow has started, turn the open end upwards as shown.)

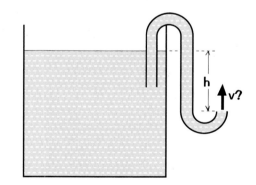

(a) Record what happens to the water as it exits the tube.

(b) How does the speed of the water depend on the height of the end of the tube below the level of the water in the container (labeled h in the diagram)? Explain. What are you using to estimate the speed of the water? How does the maximum height of the water compare to the level of the water in the container?

(c) Draw a diagram showing the trajectory of the water after it leaves the tube and the flow of water from the container until it reaches its maximum height outside the tube.

Reflection (for part A only)

R1. In situations A1, A2, and A3, does the result depend on how hard the air is blowing? Explain. Where is the air moving the fastest? the slowest? Draw diagrams showing the forces on the sheets of paper (A1) and on the ping-pong balls (A2 and A3). Where must the pressure in the moving air be the largest? the smallest? Explain.

R2. In situation A4, in which water is flowing from a hole punched in the bottom of a container, where is the water moving the fastest? the slowest? Does the speed of the escaping water depend on the amount of fluid in the container? How?

R3. In situation A5, in which a siphon draws water out of a container, how is it possible to lift water above the surface of the water in the container and over the edge of the container?

PART B: Making and Verifying Predictions

For each of the following, (a) make a prediction based on your previous experience with moving fluids, and explain why you think so. Then (b) perform a demonstration and note any differences between your prediction and the result of your demonstration.

B1. Hold a ping-pong ball inside an inverted funnel as shown.
- (a) Predict what you think will happen when you <u>blow</u> into the funnel and let go of the ball. Explain your prediction.
- (b) Demonstrate. What happened? How is the demonstration different from your prediction?

B2. Consider a container filled with water.
- (a) What do you think will happen when two very small holes are poked into the side of the container as shown, one near the top and the other near the bottom? Explain why you think so.
- (b) Demonstrate. What happened? How is the demonstration different from your prediction?

B3. Reconsider the siphon in situation A5.
- (a) How will the speed of the water depend upon the height H of the end of the tube in the water? Explain your prediction.
- (b) Demonstrate. What happened? How is the demonstration different from your prediction?

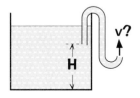

Reflection (continued)

R4. Reconsider the situations explored in this activity.

(a) How does the pressure in a fluid depend on its height? Does the pressure increase or decrease as you go higher inside the fluid? Explain why you think so.

(b) How does the pressure in a fluid depend on its speed? Does the pressure increase or decrease when the speed of the fluid becomes faster? Explain why you think so.

Integration of Ideas

BERNOULLI'S PRINCIPLE

Bernoulli's principle describes how the pressure in a fluid depends on the speed and height of a fluid, as compared to another part of the fluid. Consider the diagram to the right, which shows a pipe or tube that not only widens but also changes height.

P_a ? P_b

The pressure at point a (P_a) will be different than the pressure at point b (P_b) in part because the fluids are at different heights, but also because the fluids are moving at different speeds. When the size of the pipe stays the same, as on the left below, the speed of the fluid remains the same also. To do the work needed to get the fluid to change heights, the pressure at a must be higher than the pressure at b. When the size of the pipe changes, as on the right-hand side below, the fluid is moving slower at b. This time, to do the work needed to change the speed of the fluid, the pressure must be higher at b than at a. These results do not depend on the direction of fluid flow.

$P_a > P_b$ $\cdot b$ $a \cdot$

$P_a < P_b$ $a \cdot$ $\cdot b$

Bernoulli's principle is written:

$$P_a - P_b \ = \ \rho g\left(y_b - y_a\right) + \tfrac{1}{2}\rho\left(v_b{}^2 - v_a{}^2\right)$$ **Bernoulli's principle**

where ρ is the density of the fluid, g is the gravitational constant (e.g., 9.8N/kg on Earth), y is the height of the fluid above a common reference height, and v is the speed of the fluid at some point.

I1–8. For each of the situations above (A1–A5, B1–B3), indicate whether or not Bernoulli's principle as described here is consistent with your observations. Explain.

Analyzing Fluid Flow
with Physics Principles

Purpose and Expected Outcome

This activity is the second in a series involving moving fluids. In this activity you will apply physics principles such as Newton's laws to learn more about the dynamics of fluid flow.

Prior Experience / Knowledge Needed

You should have some experience with static fluids. You should be familiar with concepts relevant to fluids, such as *pressure*, *density*, and how the pressure changes with depth in a static fluid. You should have some experience with some common physical situations involving moving fluids.

You should also be able to apply basic principles of mechanics (such as Newton's laws and the Work–Kinetic Energy Theorem) to unfamiliar situations.

Explanation of Activity

For each of the situations described below, analyze the forces, momentum, and energy of the fluid as it flows through different shapes of pipes.

SITUATION A: Water Flowing Through Pipe with Sudden Change in Diameter

Water flows through a pipe having a 8cm diameter into a pipe having only a 4cm diameter, as shown below. 100cm^3 of water enters the larger pipe every two seconds.

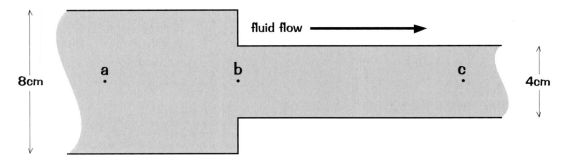

A1. (a) What is the rate at which water is flowing through the larger pipe? (Use units of volume per second.) Is the rate the same everywhere along this end of the pipe? Explain.

(b) What is the rate at which water is flowing through the smaller pipe? Is the rate the same everywhere along this end of the pipe? Explain.

(c) What principle did you use to answer part (b) above?

A2. On a copy of the drawing above, make a flow diagram for this system showing how the water flows from the larger pipe to the smaller one.

A3. Where is the speed of the water the largest, or is it the same everywhere? Explain.

A4. Compute the speed of the water in each pipe.

A5. Of the three points labeled above (*a*, *b*, and *c*), where does the fluid experience the largest net force? Explain. Where does the fluid experience the smallest net force? Explain.

A6. Consider 1 gram (1cm^3) of water as it flows through the pipe.

(a) Does its kinetic energy change anywhere in the pipe? If so, where does it change? Does its kinetic energy increase or decrease? Explain.

(b) Is work done on the water? Where? What forces do work on the water?

SITUATION B: Water Flowing Through Pipe with Gradual Change in Diameter

Water flows through a pipe having a gradually narrowing diameter, as shown below. 100cm³ of water enters the larger opening on the left every two seconds. The questions below all involve the 1cm³ of water shown surrounding point a.

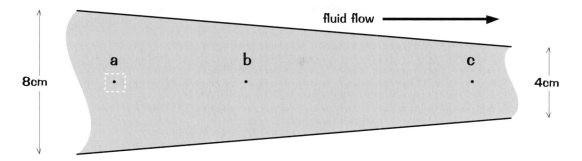

B1. On a copy of the drawing above, make a diagram for this system showing how the water flows through the pipe.

B2. As the water flows from point a to points b and c does its speed increase, decrease, or stay the same? Explain.

B3. What does your answer to B2 imply about the net force on the water? Draw a free-body diagram showing all the forces on the water.

B4. Compare the pressure in the water at points a, b, and c.

B5. Does the kinetic energy of the water change as it flows from point a to points b and c? Explain why or why not. If so, is the change positive or negative?

B6. Is work done on the water as it flows from point a to points b and c? Explain why or why not. If so, is the work positive or negative? What forces do work on the water?

SITUATION C: Water Flowing Through Siphon

A hose having a constant inner diameter of 1cm is used to siphon water out of a storage tank. Point a is just inside the hose where the water enters. Point b is at the same height as a. Point c is just inside the hose where the water exits. Questions C2 and C3 concern the 1cm^3 of water surrounding point b.

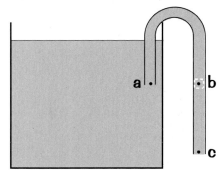

C1. Which is larger, the rate at which water enters the hose at a or the rate at which water exits the hose at c? Explain.

C2. How does the speed of the water change as it moves from point b to point c? Explain.

C3. What can you say about the net force on the water at point b? Draw a free-body diagram for the water at b.

C4. How does the pressure change between points b and c? Explain.

C5. What is the total work done on the water between points a and b? Explain.

Reflection

R1. In situation A, what idea or principle did you use to compute the speeds of the water flowing in the pipes?

R2. Reconsider situations A and B. How does the kinetic energy of the water change as it flows left to right? Does the gravitational potential energy of the water–Earth system change? What forces do work on the water?

R3. Reconsider situation C. How does the kinetic energy of the water change as it flows down the hose (after reaching its maximum height)? Does the gravitational potential energy of the water–Earth system change? What forces do work on the water?

R4. Would you say that Newton's laws apply to moving fluids? Explain. Would you say that work and energy ideas apply to moving fluids? Explain.

CS·10

Reasoning with Bernoulli's Principle

Purpose and Expected Outcome

This activity is the third in a series involving moving fluids. In this activity you will learn about *Bernoulli's principle*, the physics principle that governs the dynamics of fluid flow. You will also learn how to apply Bernoulli's principle in a variety of situations.

Prior Experience / Knowledge Needed

You should have some experience with static fluids. You should be familiar with concepts relevant to fluids, such as *pressure* and *density*. You know how the pressure changes with depth in a static fluid. You should have some experience with some common physical situations involving moving fluids.

You should have some experience with applying physics principles such as Newton's laws and the Work–Kinetic Energy Theorem to moving fluids.

BERNOULLI'S PRINCIPLE

Bernoulli's principle is a relationship between the pressure in a fluid and the speed and height of a fluid. Consider the diagram at right, which shows a pipe that not only widens but also changes height.

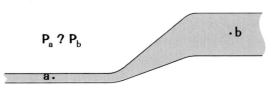

The pressure at point a (P_a) will be different than at point b (P_b) in part because the points are at different heights, but also because the fluids are moving at different speeds.

continued

When the size of the pipe stays the same, as on the left below, the speed of the fluid remains the same also. But positive work must be done to raise the fluid to point b, and the only way work can be done in this situation is if the pressure is different at a than at b. In this case, the pressure at a must be higher than the pressure at b.

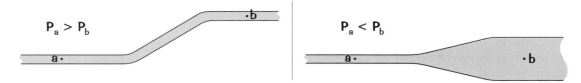

When the size of the pipe changes, as on the right-hand side above, the fluid is moving slower at b. Because the kinetic energy of the fluid is getting smaller, negative work must be done on the fluid. Therefore, even though points a and b are at the same height, to maintain fluid flow, the pressures again must be different. This time the pressure is higher at b than at a.

Bernoulli's principle is written:

$$P_a - P_b = \rho g \left(y_b - y_a \right) + \tfrac{1}{2} \rho \left(v_b{}^2 - v_a{}^2 \right) \qquad \textbf{Bernoulli's principle}$$

where ρ is the density of the fluid, g is the gravitational constant (e.g., 9.8N/kg on Earth), y is the height of the fluid above a common reference height, and v is the speed of the fluid.

Note: This relationship is true as long as the following <u>four</u> conditions are also true:

1. The flow is *steady-state*, which means that the speed of the fluid at any point along the pipe remains the same. It does not mean that the speed is the same everywhere. It means only that, for instance, the speed at point a is the same at all instants of time. The speed at another point in the pipe can be different, but it must also be constant.

2. The flow of the fluid is *streamline* or *laminar* (i.e., smooth), rather than *turbulent* (i.e., chaotic) or *circulatory* (e.g., convection currents within a room). When there are no sharp bends, kinks, or obstructions in a tube or pipe, then the flow is usually streamline. (For spinning tennis balls, baseballs, etc. and airplane wings, the flow is generally turbulent.)

3. The fluid is *incompressible*, which means that the density of the fluid is independent of the pressure in the fluid. This means also that a certain mass of fluid occupies the same volume no matter what the pressure is. (Water is nearly incompressible, while air is highly compressible.)

4. The fluid has <u>little</u> or <u>no</u> *viscosity*. This means that there is no energy loss while the fluid is flowing. Fluids must be <u>very</u> slippery to be *non-viscous*. (We generally ignore the viscosity of water.)

Explanation of Activity

For each of the situations described below, use Bernoulli's principle and your knowledge of forces, Newton's laws, work ideas, and energy ideas to analyze the situation and reason about the objects and moving fluids.

SITUATION A: Lifting a Dime Off a Table Top

A classmate arranges a dime and a shallow glass cup on a table top as shown below and claims she can get the dime into the glass cup without touching <u>anything</u>: without touching the dime; without touching the table; without touching the glass cup. The dime is entirely on the table, with no part of it hanging over the edge of the table. She further claims that no magnets, no tape, no other item at all is needed to accomplish this trick.

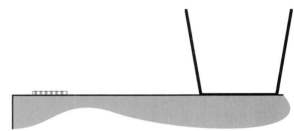

A1. How do you suppose your classmate can do what she claims? Could you do it? Devise a technique and explain why you think it might work.

A2. Arrange a dime and a shallow glass cup as shown and attempt to get the dime into the cup. Does your technique seem to be working? Describe what happens when you try.

A3. Would a different coin be better than a dime? Explain. Is there any reason why the cup must be made out of glass, or would a plastic cup work just as well as the glass cup? Is there any reason why the cup must be shallow, or would a tall glass work just as well? Explain.

SITUATION B: Watching a Stream of Water

Look at a stream of water coming out of a faucet. (Adjust the flow rate so that it is slow but steady; not dripping.)

B1. Draw a picture of the water as it flows out of the faucet and lands in the sink.

B2. Describe the shape of the stream of water. Explain the shape of the stream of water.

B3. Smoke rises. Use your observations and analysis above to predict what will happen to smoke when it rises.

SITUATION C: Blowing on a Funnel

A piece of filter paper is folded into quarters and made into a cone.
The cone is put inside a funnel turned upside down as shown.
(Everything is completely dry.)

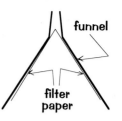

C1. Predict what will happen when someone blows into the small end of the funnel.
Explain why you think so.

C2. Try it yourself. Describe what happens. Explain.

Reflection

R1. Consider the two terms on the right-hand side of Bernoulli's principle.
(a) Show that the first term (the one involving the change in height of the fluid) has the
same units as pressure.
(b) Show that the second term (the one involving the change in the speed-squared of
the fluid) also has the same units as pressure.

R2. If the windows at the top of tall buildings are not designed properly, the glass will fall
out, risking pedestrians below. Explain why the glass might not stay in the windows.
Why is it that only tall buildings seem to have this problem?

R3. Imagine a small sample of fluid flowing through a system. The surrounding fluid does
work on the piece of fluid changing its kinetic energy and its gravitational potential
energy relative to the Earth. Which quantity in Bernoulli's equation corresponds to the
work done by the surrounding fluid? Which term corresponds to the change in kinetic
energy of the fluid? Which quantity corresponds to the change in gravitational potential
energy of the fluid–Earth system?

Solving Problems Involving Idealized Fluids

Purpose and Expected Outcome

This is the fourth is the series of activities on moving fluids. In this activity, you will learn how to apply the relationships you have learned so far to situations involving moving and static fluids. You will also learn the conditions under which a fluid or its flow may be considered *ideal*.

Prior Experience / Knowledge Needed

You should be familiar with concepts relevant to fluids, such as *density* and *pressure*. You should know how the pressure in a static fluid changes with depth. You should be familiar with Bernoulli's principle for moving fluids.

You should know Newton's laws and the Work–Kinetic Energy Theorem, and you should be able to apply them in new situations.

IDEALIZED FLUIDS

Idealized fluids obey the relationships derived or presented so far. For example, the pressure in a static fluid changes with depth according to:

$$P = P_0 + \rho g d \qquad \textbf{pressure in a static fluid at depth } \textit{d}$$

where P_0 is the pressure at the surface of the fluid and d is the depth below the surface at which the pressure is desired.

It is convenient to rewrite this relationship by considering two points at different depths, as shown to the right. Applying the previous relationship at each point, we get the following two equations:

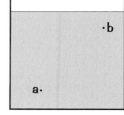

$$P_a = P_0 + \rho g d_a \qquad\qquad P_b = P_0 + \rho g d_b$$

Subtracting the right equation from the left equation and combining terms, we get:

$$P_a - P_b = \rho g \left(d_a - d_b \right)$$

The difference in the depths may be rewritten using the difference in the heights to get:

$$P_a - P_b = \rho g \left(y_b - y_a \right) \qquad \textbf{pressure difference between two points in a static fluid}$$

Note that this relationship is equivalent to Bernoulli's principle when the fluid is at rest:

$$P_a - P_b = \rho g \left(y_b - y_a \right) + \tfrac{1}{2} \rho \left(v_b{}^2 - v_a{}^2 \right) \qquad \textbf{Bernoulli's principle}$$

Thus, Bernoulli's principle may be applied to both moving and static fluids. An idealized fluid (or its flow) has the following four properties:

1. An idealized fluid is *incompressible*, which means that the density of the fluid is independent of the pressure in the fluid. This means also that a certain mass of fluid occupies the same volume no matter what the pressure is. (Water is nearly incompressible, while air is highly compressible.)

2. An idealized fluid has <u>little</u> or <u>no</u> *viscosity*. This means that there is no energy loss while the fluid is flowing. Fluids must be <u>very</u> slippery to be *non-viscous*. (We generally ignore the viscosity of water.)

3. The flow of an idealized fluid is *streamline* or *laminar*, rather than *turbulent* or *circulatory*. When there are no sharp bends, kinks, or obstructions in a tube or pipe, then the flow is usually streamline. (For spinning balls and airplane wings, the flow is generally turbulent.)

4. The flow of an idealized fluid is *steady-state*, which means that the pressure and speed is constant in time at every point in the fluid.

Explanation of Activity

In each of the problems below, you may assume that Bernoulli's principle applies. Use as atmospheric pressure 100kPa (1kPa = 1000N/m²) or 10N/cm² throughout. Also assume that 10cm³ of oil has a mass of 9g. Be prepared to explain your answers.

A1. Water is poured into a *U-tube* as shown. Determine the pressure at each of the five points labeled in the diagram.

(a) At the surface of the water on the left-hand side.

(b) Near the side of the tube, as shown.

(c) In the middle of the U, as shown.

(d) In the U, but on the right-hand side, as shown.

(e) In the middle of the right-hand side of the tube, as shown.

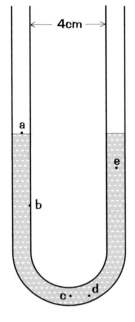

A2. Consider situation A1, in which a U-tube is partially filled with water. Oil is poured into the right-hand side of the tube until it occupies a 10cm-long section of the tube.

(a) Draw the new situation.

(b) Determine the locations of the upper surfaces of fluid and the location of the oil/water interface.

(c) Determine the pressure in the right-hand side of the tube at the same height as the surface of the water in the left-hand side.

A3. A glass tube with a square cross-section is partially filled with water as shown to the right. The inner sides of the tube measure 1cm along each edge. One end of the tube is closed, and the other end is open.

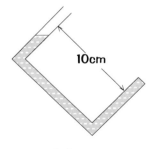

(a) The tube is rotated so that it rests on its side. Draw this <u>new</u> situation.

(b) What volume of water is in the tube?

(c) What is the pressure at the surface of the water on the right-hand side?

(d) What is the pressure just inside the top of the closed end of the tube?

continued

A4. A closed pipe with a 1cm inner diameter has a small (1mm) hole drilled into its end as shown. The pipe is filled with water, which is allowed to escape through the hole. The pressure inside the pipe, far from the hole, is maintained at twice atmospheric pressure (i.e., $P =$ 200kPa = 20N/cm^2).

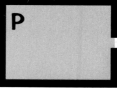

(a) What is the pressure in the water just outside the hole?

(b) What is the speed of the water as it exits the hole?

(c) How would your answers change if oil is used instead?

(d) How would your answers change if the hole was in the bottom of the pipe instead of its end?

A5. A siphon is used to remove water from a small tank as shown. One end of the siphon is at depth d = 4cm, and the other end is at height h = 6cm below the surface of the water.

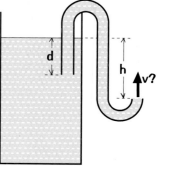

(a) What is the speed v of the water as it exits the tube?

(b) What is the maximum height of the water after it leaves the tube?

(c) Draw this situation, showing the trajectory of the water after it leaves the tube.

(d) Sketch a graph of the speed v of the water as it exits the hole vs. time t.

(e) What is the minimum speed v that occurs in this situation?

Reflection

R1. How would your answers to the following questions change if the system is put into a vacuum? Explain.

(a) Question A1(a)–(e), in which a U-tube is partially filled with water.

(b) Question A3(a), in which a tube with one closed end is partially filled with water.

(c) Question A4(b), in which a small hole is drilled into the end of a closed pipe.

R2. Reconsider situation A2, in which oil is added to a U-tube with water. How would your answer to part (b) change if the system is on the surface of the Moon? Explain.

R3. What is the most difficult part of applying Bernoulli's principle? What are your most common mistakes when applying Bernoulli's principle? Why do you suppose you make these mistakes?

CS·12

Exploring Other Fluid Phenomena

Purpose and Expected Outcome

Real fluids can lead to a wide range of complex behavior. The fluid principles developed so far are not enough to explain everything. In this activity you will examine a range of fluid situations, only some of which can be understood using the fluid principles you know. When you find a system that you cannot apply a known fluid principle you can always use Newton's laws to reason about the situation.

Prior Experience / Knowledge Needed

You should be familiar with concepts relevant to fluids, such as *density* and *pressure*. You should know how the pressure in a static fluid changes with depth. You should be familiar with Bernoulli's principle for moving fluids.

You should know Newton's laws and the Work–Kinetic Energy Theorem, and you should be able to apply them in new situations.

Explanation of Activity

In each of the following situations, use fluid principles to explain the described phenomenon. If fluid principles fail to apply, use Newton's laws or energy ideas to explain the behavior of the system.

A1. A diver plans to breathe through a tube open to air at the surface of the lake. Evaluate this technique.

A2. (a) Imagine a tank of water with a hole in its side near the bottom. Will the water come out with a greater speed with a small hole or large hole? Explain, then verify what actually happens.

(b) What happens when you place your finger over the end of a garden hose (without completely blocking the flow of water) while the water is turned on? Is this consistent with what you found above in part (a)? Explain any contradictions.

A3. Bernoulli's principle is often used to explain part of the lift on the wing of an airplane. How would you explain lift using Bernoulli's principle? Will the lift on an airplane depend on the altitude of the plane? Explain. (Make sure you state any assumptions you make.)

A4. A tornado will lift heavy objects, tear roofs off of buildings, and cause windows to explode outward.

(a) Explain these observations.

(b) Estimate the pressure in the interior of a tornado. Estimate wind velocities assuming Bernoulli's equation is valid.

(c) Comment on the validity and applicability of Bernoulli's equation.

A5. Razor blades sink when placed in the water. Nevertheless, a razor blade carefully placed on the surface of water will "float". How would you explain these observations? Draw a free-body diagram for the case where the razor blade is "floating" on top of the water.

Reflection

R1. At least one of the conditions necessary for Bernoulli's principle is not true for flowing air. Which one(s)? Explain why you think so.

R2. Reconsider situation A1, in which a diver breathes through a tube open to the air above the surface of the water. Describe a method for allowing the diver to breathe normally.

R3. Consider the device shown below. A glass container is made with a spout that is open to the air and a large reservoir. The reservoir is partially filled with water when the container is on its back, as on the left. The container is then slowly turned so that it is vertical, as on the right.

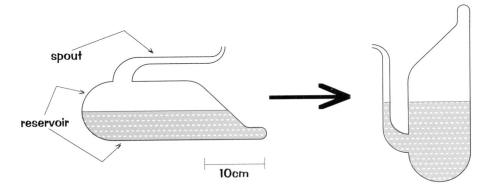

(a) Are the levels of water in the spout and in the reservoir <u>necessarily</u> the same? Explain. Under what conditions will the levels be different?

(b) Under what conditions will the level of the water in the spout change? Do you think it is even possible for the level of the water in the spout to change?

(c) On a particular day, water is observed to be spilling out of the end of the spout. What can you say about the conditions outside this device? What can you say about the conditions inside the reservoir above the water line?

(d) As conditions cause the water level in the spout to move up and down, what happens to the water level in the reservoir? Which level changes more? Explain. What can you say about the pressure inside the reservoir as the water level in the spout moves up and down?

Exploring Heat
and Temperature

Purpose and Expected Outcome

The ideas of *temperature* and *heat* are explored in this activity. The objective is to refine your understanding of how to use and to apply these terms. The distinction between these terms should be clearer after completing this activity.

Prior Experience / Knowledge Needed

No previous knowledge or experience is needed to do this activity.

Explanation of Activity

There are two parts in this activity. In the first part, you will record your observations and reflections about situations involving *temperature*. In the second part, you will focus on the idea of *heat*.

PART A: Sensing Temperature

Carefully record your ideas, observations, and sensations as you work through each of the following items.

A1. What does it mean to say that something is *hot*? ... that something is *cold*? Is being hot the presence or absence of something? Why do you think that?

A2. Fill a container about half full of warm water from the tap. Measure the temperature of the water using a thermometer. Insert a finger into the water. Describe your sensation. Repeat this process using some cold water.

A3. Fill two containers half full with water. Use very warm water (not too hot!) for one and cold water for the other. Fill a third container half full with water at room temperature. Place your fingers from your left hand into the very warm water. Place your fingers from your right hand into the cold water. Wait about 30 seconds. Now place the fingers from both hands in the room temperature water. Describe what you feel.

A4. Hold your hand in contact with a large piece of metal that has been sitting in the room for a long time, such as a pipe or metal desk. How does it feel? What temperature do you estimate that it is? Repeat this process with a piece of cloth. Record your estimates and sensations. Measure the temperature by placing a thermometer in contact with the two substances. Do the measured values of the temperature agree with your estimates? Explain why or why not.

A5. Hold your hand in front of your mouth and exhale slowly while keeping your mouth wide open. Describe how your breath feels on your hand. What temperature do you estimate that your breath is? Now blow across your hand. Describe how this feels and how it is different from your previous description. What temperature do you estimate that your breath is? Record your estimates and sensations. Measure the temperature of your breath by exhaling slowly onto a thermometer. Measure the temperature of your breath by blowing quickly onto a thermometer. Do the measured values of the temperature agree with your estimates? Explain any differences.

Reflection (for part A only)

R1. Consider question A3. Is your sense of temperature more reliable in some situations than in others? Explain.

R2. Consider question A4. Is it temperature that we sense when our skin is in contact with something? Or is it something else that we sense? Explain. Under what conditions is our sense of temperature reliable?

PART B: Investigating Heat

Carefully record your predictions, observations, and sensations as you work through each of the following items.

B1. Measure the temperature of your hand by placing the bulb of a thermometer in contact with the palm of your open hand. Now rub your hands back and forth vigorously for about 10 seconds, then touch your cheeks. How does it feel? Do you think a thermometer would measure the temperature of your palm now to be different than it was before? Explain your reasoning.

B2. Blow through a straw across the back of your hand. How does it feel? Wet the back of your hand with some water. Again blow across the back of your hand. How does it feel now? Is there any difference? Explain.

B3. Blow through a straw and allow the air from the end of the straw to hit a thermometer bulb. After the thermometer has stopped changing, record the temperature. Wet the thermometer bulb with water. Again blow through a straw across the thermometer bulb. What is the reading now? Is the reading different? Explain. Are these readings consistent with your sensations observed in B2?

B4. Take a headless nail, lay it down on something hard and hit it with a hammer several times. Place the nail in your hand. How does it feel? Do you think a thermometer would measure the temperature of the nail now to be different than it was before? Explain your reasoning.

B5. Drive a headless nail part way into a piece of wood. Touch the nail with your hand. How does it feel? Do you think a thermometer would measure the temperature of the nail now to be different than it was before? Explain.

Reflection (continued)

R3. In which situations in part B did the temperature change? What caused this change?

R4. A thermometer measures temperature. But, what do you think temperature is? Or, what do you think determines the temperature of something?

R5. Why do weather forecasts in the winter often provide a "wind-chill" temperature? What does this temperature represent? Under what conditions is the "wind-chill" temperature the same as the air temperature?

R6. Why do weather forecasts in the summer sometimes provide a "heat index"? Under what conditions is the heat index higher than the air temperature? What does this temperature represent?

Summary

The above examples should make it clear that our perception of temperature is inaccurate and subjective. Furthermore, in everyday language we do not use the term *heat* very precisely. We sometimes use the term to refer to a form of energy and sometimes we use the term to describe the transfer of energy. Our body is constantly engaging in a variety of chemical processes that generate excess energy usually called *heat*. We have a comfortable range of body temperatures and regulate our environment to maintain our temperature in that range. Under normal circumstances this regulation requires that we release thermal energy at a significant rate.

Our human senses are extremely sensitive to the transfer of energy. We feel cold when we lose thermal energy too quickly and feel hot when we do not lose thermal energy quickly enough. This is why metal, which is a good thermal energy conductor (just as it is a good electrical conductor), feels cool to the touch even when it is at room temperature. Even though both the air and the metal are at room temperature, energy is transferred from your hand to the metal more quickly than to the air, so the metal feels cooler. This is also why blowing through a straw at your hand feels cool, but blowing through the straw at a thermometer will raise the temperature from room temperature. Your breath is actually warmer than your hand, but when you blow on your hand, the moving air can carry energy away, cooling your hand slightly.

Investigating Thermal Equilibrium

Purpose and Expected Outcome

Thermal equilibrium is an essential concept needed to understand the process of temperature change. This concept is explored in this activity. When you are finished, you will understand better the factors that affect how temperature changes.

Prior Experience / Knowledge Needed

You should be familiar with the concept of energy and its basic forms, *kinetic* and *potential*. You should also be familiar with the ideas of *macroscopic* and *microscopic* energy. You should know the law of Conservation of Energy and you should be able to apply it in unfamiliar situations.

Explanation of Activity

In Part A you will predict the outcome of a few simple experiments. In part B you will do the experiments and check whether your predictions are correct.

PART A: Predicting the Results of Mixing

Record your predictions for the outcome of each of the following experiments. In each case explain your reasoning.

A1. One cup of water at 50°C is mixed with one cup of water at 20°C. After the mixture comes to equilibrium what will be its temperature? In other words, when the reading on your thermometer seems to stop changing, what temperature will it read?

A2. One cup of water at 60°C is mixed with one cup of water at 15°C. After the mixture comes to equilibrium what will be its temperature?

A3. One cup of water at 50°C is mixed with one cup of water at 20°C. One cup of this mixture is then mixed with another cup of water at 20°C. After the second mixture comes to equilibrium what will be its final temperature?

A4. One cup of water at 40°C, one cup of water at 20°C, and one cup of water at 15°C are mixed together. After the mixture comes to equilibrium what will be its final temperature?

A5. One cup of water at 50°C is mixed with two cups of water at 20°C. After the final mixture comes to equilibrium what will be the final temperature?

A6. One cup of water at 50°C is mixed with 9 cups of water at 20°C. What will be the final temperature of this mixture?

A7. A piece of aluminum which has been sitting for a long time in water at 20°C. The metal weighs as much as a cup of water. The metal is placed in a container and one cup of water at 50°C is poured on top. Do you expect the final temperature of the metal and water to be higher than, lower than, or the same as the final temperature in A1 (in which one cup of water at 20°C is mixed with one cup of water at 50°C)? Explain your reasoning.

PART B: Measuring the Results of Mixing

In this part you will determine experimentally the answers to the situations in Part A. You will need a source of warm and cold water, a thermometer, some measuring cups, and a mixing container. It is better if the cups and mixing container are made of STYROFOAM* as this material does not transmit heat readily. You should always measure the initial temperature of your water by filling the cups and then waiting about a minute before measuring the temperatures. Conversely, after pouring the water into the mixing container, you should measure the temperature right away.

B1. Fill one cup with warm tap water and another with cool tap water. Measure the temperature of each and record your measurements. Pour both cups into your mixing container and measure the temperature immediately. Is this the temperature that you expected? Explain if your result is not in agreement with your answers to A1 and A2.

B2. Discard one cup of your mixture from B1. After measuring its temperature, pour another cup of cool tap water into the container and measure the temperature immediately. Is this the temperature that you expected? Explain if your result is not in agreement with your answer to A3.

B3. Fill one cup with very warm water, one cup with cold water, and another cup with a mixture of warm and cold water. After measuring the temperatures in all the cups, pour them into the mixing container and measure the temperature immediately. Is this the temperature that you expected? Explain if your result is not in agreement with your answer to A4.

B4. Fill two cups with cool tap water and one with warm tap water. After measuring the temperatures in all the cups, pour them into the mixing container and measure the temperature immediately. Is this the temperature that you expected? Explain if your result is not in agreement with your answer to A5.

B5. Allow a piece of aluminum that weighs about the same as a cup of water to sit a long time in cool water. The time should be at least 5 minutes. It may be necessary to change the water several times to make sure that all the metal is at the temperature of the water. Fill a cup with very warm water. Measure the temperature of both cups of water. Place the cooled metal alone in the mixing container and pour in the cup of warm water. Measure the temperature immediately, but also repeatedly over the next few minutes. Is the final temperature warmer or cooler than the temperature measured in B1? Is this result as you expected and in accord with your answer in A7? Explain any difference. What might have caused the difference?

* Trademark of The Dow Chemical Company

Reflection

R1. What does the term *equilibrium* mean when used in the context of temperature? What is *thermal equilibrium*?

R2. Why is it a good idea to wait a little while to measure the temperature of your cups of water?

R3. Why is it a good idea to have a mixing container made out of STYROFOAM?

R4. Why should you measure the temperature of the mixture of water immediately?

R5. Consider B5. What would happen if you were to use half as much metal? Would the final temperature be the same as, higher than, or lower than the temperature measured in B5? Explain.

R6. What do you think would happen if you could put two identical pieces of metal together, one at 20°C and the other at 50°C? What would be the final temperature?

Integration of Ideas

I1. Ten grams of water at 20°C is mixed with 20 grams of water at 50°C. What is the final temperature of the mixture?

I2. Ten grams of oil at 20°C is mixed with 20 grams of oil at 50°C. What is the final temperature of the mixture?

I3. n grams of water at 20°C is mixed with m grams of water at 50°C. What is the final temperature of the mixture? (Verify your result using your answer to I1.)

I4. n grams of water at T_1 is mixed with m grams of water at T_2. What is the final temperature of the mixture? (Verify your result using your answer to I1.)

Summary

When two systems are in contact, *thermal equilibrium* is reached when they are at the same temperature. In other words, the two systems will exchange energy until they both have the same temperature.

Heat is the term we use to refer to the microscopic energy transferred from one system to another. The standard unit of energy for heat is the *calorie* (cal). By definition, it takes about 1cal of heat to raise the temperature of 1g of water by 1°C. One calorie is equal to about 4.2J. In other words, it takes the same amount of energy to raise a 0.42kg object by 1m (work = 4.2J) as it does to raise the temperature of 1g of water by 1°C (heat = 1cal).

Different substances require different amounts of energy to change their temperatures. The amount of heat needed to change 1g of a substance by 1°C is called its *specific heat*. For instance, the specific heat of aluminum is about 1/5 cal/g·°C, and the specific heat of copper is about 1/10 cal/g·°C. This means, for example, that when water and aluminum at different temperatures are in contact with each other, as heat is exchanged between the two, the aluminum will experience a change in temperature that is about 5 times that of the water, because its specific heat is about 1/5 as large as that of water.

The specific heat also depends on the temperature of the substance, but only slightly in most cases, so we often treat the specific heat as a constant or as an average value. For instance, the specific heat of water is about 1.007cal/g·°C at 0°C, about 0.998cal/g·°C at 33°C, and about 1.004cal/g·°C at 74°C. The specific heat of a substance can also depend on other factors, such as pressure.

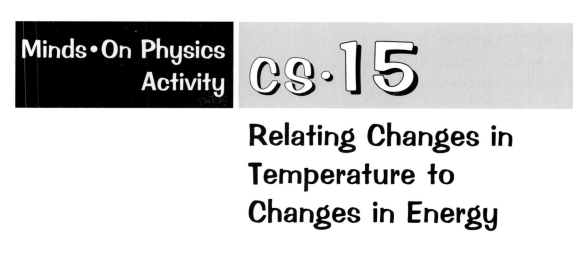

Relating Changes in Temperature to Changes in Energy

Purpose and Expected Outcome

You will examine the energy changes in systems and analyze their effect on the temperature, pressure and volume of a system.

Prior Experience / Knowledge Needed

You should have completed the previous activity and be familiar with the concepts of work and energy. In particular, you should be familiar with the idea of microscopic energy, and you should have some experience with processes that change the amount of energy in the microscopic realm, such as a block sliding on a rough surface.

HEAT VS. WORK

The energy of a system can change only if the system interacts with its environment, such that work is done on the system. We want to apply this concept at the microscopic level. You may have already learned the *atomic model*. All material, whether gas, liquid, or solid, consists of a large number of individual atoms, all interacting with each other. Work is done at the macroscopic level by applying a force through a displacement, as in compressing a gas with a piston. At the microscopic level, work is done by an individual molecule when it collides with others. It is impossible to keep track of the work done at the microscopic level using our definition. It is customary to refer to the energy exchanged in this way as *heat*.

Work, whether by a macroscopic applied force or by microscopic collisions, is the only way that energy can enter or leave a <u>closed</u> system. This latter process is often referred to as *heat conduction*. It is important to distinguish this process from other heat transfer processes that you may have learned about, such as *convection* and *radiation*. In those processes the system is not closed.

Explanation of Activity

For each of the problems below, a situation or action is described and a system is defined. In each case, consider the changes in energy and/or temperature of the system. If the energy or temperature of the system has changed, indicate whether it has increased or decreased. In some cases, indicate the mechanism(s) involved in any changes in energy.

A1. Rub your hands together. Consider your hands as the system.

(a) Has the energy of your hands changed? Has their temperature changed? How?

(b) What mechanism is responsible for any change in energy?

A2. A container of gas is opened in a vacuum and the gas is allowed to expand into a larger container. Consider the gas.

(a) Has the energy of the gas changed? Has its temperature changed? How?

(b) What mechanism is responsible for any change in energy?

A3. Squeeze a balloon filled with air. Consider the balloon.

(a) Has work been done on the balloon? Has the energy of the balloon changed? Has its temperature changed? Indicate the directions (up or down) of any changes.

(b) What mechanism is responsible for any change in energy? Where does the energy come from? Where does the energy go?

A4. A cup of cold water is placed in a large bowl as shown and warm water is poured into the bowl so that it surrounds the cup. Consider the cup of cold water over some period of time.

(a) Has the energy of the cup of water changed? Sketch the energy of the cup of water vs. time. How do you know whether or not there has been a change?

(b) If the energy has changed, what processes were involved to cause these changes?

continued

A5. A piece of hot metal is placed in cold water. Does the metal or the water experience the larger temperature change? Which experiences the larger energy change? Explain. Describe the mechanism for the energy change.

A6. Consider your own body. As you engage in normal activities is your temperature changing? Is your energy changing? Would your answers be the same if you were out in the hot sunshine and then jumped into a cool pool of water?

A7. A cloud passes and allows bright sunlight to hit the blacktop of a parking lot. Does the energy of the blacktop change? How do you know? Does the temperature of the blacktop change? If the temperature changes, what factors affect the amount of change?

A8. A cube of ice at 0°C melts in water that is also at 0°C. Does either the ice or the water have a change in temperature? Does either have a change in energy? If any changes occur, which has the larger change?

A9. A piece of iron that is red hot is removed from a fire and allowed to cool in air.
   (a) Does the energy of the iron change?
   (b) By what process does it change?

A10. Increasing the pressure on a gas will cause it to become a liquid without cooling the material.
   (a) Does the temperature of this substance change? Does its energy?
   (b) What processes are involved in any change of these quantities?

Reflection

R1. Is it possible for the energy of something to change without its temperature changing? If so, give some examples. If not, explain why not.

R2. Is it possible for the temperature of something to change without its energy changing? If so, give some examples. If not, explain why not.

R3. Your body employs a variety of physical processes in its attempt to regulate your temperature. List all such processes that you can think of, and for each, discuss its relative importance for temperature regulation.

R4. What attributes of an object do you think would affect the amount of heat that could be conducted through the object?

R5. What attributes of an object would affect the amount of energy that can be radiated by the object?

Summary

Thermal equilibrium means that the objects in contact have the same temperature. If there is a temperature difference, energy will flow from one object to the other until their temperatures are the same. *Heat* is a form of microscopic work that is performed by the constituents as they undergo their random motions, colliding with other atoms near them.

In other words, the colder object is heated by the warmer object, because energy flows from the warmer object to the colder one, until they are at the same temperature. The amount of energy that flows out of the warmer object is equal to the amount of energy that flows into the colder one. When the two objects reach the same temperature, the net energy flow is zero.

CS·16

Exploring the Concept of Energy in Complex Systems

Purpose and Expected Outcome

The systems that you analyzed earlier in the course contained only a few objects. Newton's Laws of Motion are most easily applied only when the number of interacting bodies are few and when they have no moving parts. Real objects often contain many components that we wish to treat as a single system. In this activity we will explore some *complex systems* to see how Newtonian principles of mechanics may still be applied.

Prior Experience / Knowledge Needed

You need to be familiar with Newton's Laws of Motion. While these laws are not enough to solve every problem, they go a long way in helping you to analyze a situation in terms of the forces present. You should be able to determine the work done by common forces, and you should know the definition of potential energy. In particular, you should be comfortable with the Work–Kinetic Energy Theorem and Conservation of Energy.

Although the previous activities in this section are not directly related to this one, it is useful to keep in mind the overall goal. This goal is to perceive the role of energy in complex systems and how the thermodynamic quantity *temperature* can be related to this internal energy.

COMPLEX SYSTEMS

A *complex system* is defined to be a system of interacting objects for which it is not practical to consider the forces on individual objects. Usually, complex systems are composed of a very large number of atoms and molecules. We find that even though Newton's laws are impractical to apply, many properties of a complex system can be determined or predicted, such as the average kinetic energy per object in the system.

Explanation of Activity

In this activity you will study two models of complex systems. The first is a sequence of coupled pendulums. The second is a set of pucks on an air table.

MODEL A: Simple and Coupled Pendulums

Each simple pendulum is made using about 1 foot of light string and a heavy, metal nut. Each one is tied firmly to a horizontal string between two posts about 18 inches apart. Arrange the pendulums symmetrically between the two posts and allow the system to come to rest. Pull one of the nuts towards you at an angle of about 30° and release it from rest. Observe the behavior. Even though the energy in the system eventually dissipates, answer the questions as though the system retains <u>all</u> of its energy.

A1. Simple Pendulum. This system consists of one pendulum placed in the middle of the horizontal string.

(a) Just before the release, in what form is the energy of the nut?

(b) When the nut reaches the lowest point in its swing, in what form is the energy?

(c) On the same set of axes, make a rough sketch of the kinetic energy and the potential energy of the nut as functions of time.

(d) Let E_{max} be the total energy of the nut. Looking at several swings, what do you estimate the average of the kinetic energy to be? ... of the potential energy?

A2. Coupled Double Pendulum. This system consists of two identical simple pendulums arranged symmetrically as shown. Pull one pendulum towards you, while allowing the other to hang freely.

(a) Just before the release, in what form is all the energy in the system?

(b) On one set of axes, sketch the kinetic energies of the two nuts as functions of time.

(c) Let E_{max} be the total energy in the system. Looking at several cycles of the system, what is the average of the kinetic energy? ... of the potential energy?

(d) Let E_1 be the total energy of the first nut. What is the average value of E_1?

(e) What fraction of the total energy in the system is the average of the kinetic energy of the first nut? ... of the potential energy of the first nut?

continued

A3. Coupled Triple Pendulum. This system consists of three identical simple pendulums arranged symmetrically as shown. Pull one of the nuts toward you, while allowing the others to hang freely.

(a) Does the long term behavior depend upon which of the nuts you displace and release?

(b) Let E_{max} be the total energy in the system. What is the average of all of the kinetic energy in the system?

(c) Let E_1 be the total energy of the first nut. What is the average value of E_1?

(d) What fraction of the total energy in the system is the average of the kinetic energy of the first nut? ... is the average of the potential energy of the first nut?

A4. Coupled Quintuple Pendulum. This system consists of five identical simple pendulums arranged symmetrically as shown. Pull one of the nuts toward you, while allowing the others to hang freely.

(a) Let E_{max} be the total amount of energy in the system. What is the average of all of the kinetic energy in the system?

(b) Let E_1 be the total energy of the first nut. What is the average of E_1?

(c) What fraction of the total energy in the system is the average of the kinetic energy of the first nut?

(d) Would your answers to (b) and (c) be different for one of the other nuts? Explain.

(e) Does the average behavior depend upon which nut you pull towards you and release?

A5. Suppose a very large number of identical pendulums were suspended from the top string. Let N represent this number. Assume that one of the nuts is displaced and released from rest.

(a) Let E_{max} be the total amount of energy in the system. What is the average of all of the kinetic energy in the system?

(b) What is the average of the total energy of any one of the pendulums?

(c) What is the average of the kinetic energy of any one of the pendulums?

MODEL B: Pucks on an Air Table

Imagine an air table with rigid walls that has a large number (N) of identical pucks of mass m, all of which are motionless but randomly distributed over the surface of the table as shown to the left below.

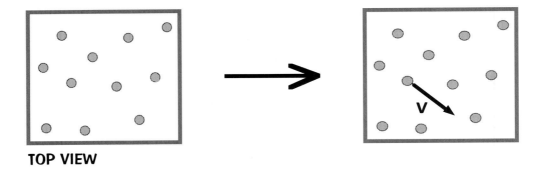

TOP VIEW

Suppose that one of the pucks is given an impulse, so that it has kinetic energy $E_K = 1/2mv^2$ as shown above to the right. Assume that there is no interaction between the pucks other than a contact force experienced during a collision. All the pucks collide with each other and the walls of the table *elastically*; in other words, no energy is lost. Assume that sufficient time has passed that there has been a very large number of collisions.

B1.   What is the total energy of the system?

B2.   What is the average energy of each puck?

B3.   What is the average speed of each puck?

B4.   What is the total momentum of the system?

B5.   What is the average velocity of each puck?

Reflection

R1. Compare the two models. How are they similar? What is one major difference between them?

R2. (a) Is either of the models (A or B) appropriate for describing gases. Which one? Why do you think so? What is one major difference between the model and the actual behavior of gases?

(b) Is either of the models (A or B) appropriate for describing solids. Which one? Why do you think so?

R3. For any particular system, what is the average total kinetic energy plus the average total potential energy? Explain. Does this result relate to any fundamental principle you have studied? Explain.

R4. In A1(c), how did the average kinetic energy compare with the average potential energy? Would the same relationship hold for a superball dropped from height h which loses no energy when it bounces? (**Hint:** Sketch the kinetic energy vs. time, and consider how much time the ball spends above height $h/2$.)

R5. Consider an alternative model to that of model A. In this model, a large set of masses are connected together with springs. Would your answers to A5 be the same or different for this system? Explain.

CS·17

Relating Thermal Motion and Temperature

Purpose and Expected Outcome

One of the models investigated in the previous activity was a collection of pucks confined to an air table. You have seen that the internal energy of this complex system is all in the form of kinetic energy of the individual particles. This model is analogous to a model that is often applied to gases. The relationship between the internal energy of a set of point particles and temperature will be explored in this activity.

Prior Experience / Knowledge Needed

To benefit from this activity you should have a good command of Newton's laws and the concepts of *force*, *momentum*, and *energy*. You also should have some experience with the concepts of *temperature*, *heat*, and *thermal equilibrium*.

THE PERFECT (OR IDEAL) GAS LAW

You may have encountered the *Perfect Gas Law* previously in a physical science or chemistry course. (Sometimes it is called the *Ideal Gas Law*.) It is an empirical relationship between the pressure (P), volume (V), temperature (T), and number of moles (n) of a gas. It can be shown experimentally that a linear relationship exists between the quantity PV/n and the temperature T. Mathematically, it may be written:

$$\frac{PV}{n} = RT + \text{constant}$$ **Perfect Gas Law**

R is called the *Universal Gas Constant*, and T can be measured using <u>any</u> temperature scale (such as Centigrade or Fahrenheit). The constant depends on which scale you use.

continued

THE KELVIN TEMPERATURE SCALE

There are two commonly used temperature scales, the Fahrenheit scale and the Centigrade scale. As you may already know these scales are defined by assigning specific numerical values for the freezing and boiling points of pure water, and then by dividing the scale into some particular number of intervals. For example, the Centigrade scale assigns 0 to the freezing point and 100 to the boiling point (of water), while the Fahrenheit scale assigns 32 to the freezing point and 212 to the boiling point (of water).

The *Kelvin* temperature scale is defined using a gas thermometer. Because gases (especially dilute gases) obey the Perfect Gas Law, when the volume and number of moles of gas are constant, pressure vs. temperature is a straight line, as shown by the solid line in the graph below.

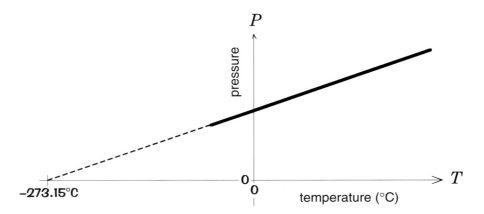

If we extend the straight line to smaller and smaller temperatures and pressures, we reach a limit for how cold the gas can be. This occurs at –273.15°C, which is often referred to as *absolute zero*, because this is the zero point of the Kelvin temperature scale. Also, a change of one degree on the Kelvin scale is the same as that for the Centigrade scale, so the relationship between the temperatures on the two scales is given by:

$$T_K = T_C + 273.15$$ **conversion from Centigrade to Kelvin temperature**

We can rewrite the Perfect Gas Law using the Kelvin scale to be:

$$\frac{PV}{n} = RT_K$$ **Perfect Gas Law using the Kelvin temperature scale**

or in its more familiar form:

$$PV = nRT_K$$ **Perfect Gas Law using the Kelvin temperature scale**

where now the temperature <u>must</u> be measured using the Kelvin scale.

Explanation of Activity

The concepts and principles of Newtonian mechanics are used to analyze the behavior of an ideal gas of point particles. In the first part of this activity, we will take as our system a fixed rigid box containing a single gas particle. In the second part, the system is a cylindrical container with a very large number of non-interacting gas particles.

PART A: Force on a Wall by a Single Particle

Consider a cubic box with sides of length d. Suppose there is a single gas particle of mass m inside this box. Assume that initially the gas particle is traveling in the positive x-direction with velocity v_x. The speed of the gas particle is so large that the particle crosses the box many times every second.

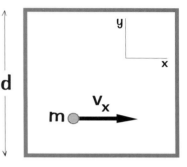

A1. What is the initial momentum of the particle?

A2. The particle collides and rebounds from the right wall with the same speed (in other words, without losing any energy). What impulse has been delivered to the right wall of the box by the gas particle?

A3. How long does it take the particle to travel the width of the box?

A4. In one second, how many times will the particle strike the right wall of the box?

A5. During the one second, what is the total impulse the particle delivers to the right wall of the box?

A6. What is the average force on the right wall of the box?

Summary of part A

Each time a gas particle hits a wall or other surface, it exerts a (relatively) large normal force for a very short period of time. The wall also exerts a force, which delivers the impulse needed to change the gas particle's momentum. The impulse delivered every time the particle hits a wall is $J = 2mv_x$, and the time between collisions with the wall is $\Delta t = 2d/v_x$. Therefore, the average force is $F_{ave} = J/\Delta t = 2mv_x/(2d/v_x) = mv_x^2/d$, and the pressure due to a single gas particle hitting either one of the walls (area = d^2) is:

$$P = \frac{F_{ave}}{d^2} = \frac{mv_x^2}{d^3}$$

pressure on the left and right walls of the box due to <u>one</u> gas particle

When the motion of the gas particle is not limited only to the x-direction, the pressure on the left or right wall of the box still depends <u>only</u> on the x-component of velocity v_x.

When there are many particles inside the box, we simply add the forces together to get the total force exerted by all the particles. Still, the pressure on the left or right wall of the box depends only on the x-components of the velocities of all the particles in the box:

$$P = \frac{mv_{1x}^2 + mv_{2x}^2 + ... + mv_{Nx}^2}{d^3}$$

pressure on the left and right walls of the box due to <u>many</u> gas particles

where N is the total number of gas particles in the box, and v_{1x} is the x-component of the first gas particle, v_{2x} is the x-component of the second gas particle, etc.

The numerator on the right-hand side above <u>looks</u> like the total kinetic energy, but not quite. First, it is missing a factor of $1/2$. Second, it is missing contributions from the y- and z-components of velocity. (Keep in mind that the box is three-dimensional.) We can say, however, that the total kinetic energy has equal contributions due to components in the x-, y-, and z-directions. Therefore, the numerator above is equal to $2/3 E_{K,total}$.

The denominator on the right-hand side above is the volume of the box, so the relationship may be rearranged to get:

$$PV = \frac{2}{3} E_{K,total}$$

relationship between pressure, volume, and total kinetic energy

Now, using the Perfect Gas Law, we can relate the total kinetic energy in a perfect gas to the temperature of the gas:

$$E_{K,total} = \frac{3}{2} nRT_K$$

total kinetic energy in a perfect gas at temperature T_K

Note that the two "K" subscripts above refer to different features: the "kinetic" energy and the "Kelvin" temperature scale. Note also that this relationship is true for any size and shape of box.

PART B: Reasoning About Perfect Gases

Consider a cylindrical container with a very large number N of identical gas particles in it. A piston having mass M and area A is positioned as shown, and it is free to slide up and down inside the cylinder. The original volume of the cylinder is V, and the original temperature of the gas is not known.

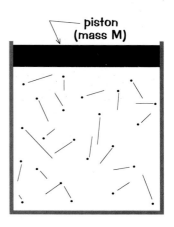

For each of the questions below, reason through to an answer using either kinematics, Newton's laws, definitions of basic physical quantities, conservation laws, the Perfect Gas Law, or the relationship just derived for the total kinetic energy of a gas at temperature T_K. Be prepared to explain your answers.

B1. In terms of the known quantities given above and other known quantities...

(a) ... what is the total inner surface area of the cylinder?

(b) ... how many moles of gas are in the container?

(c) ... what is the temperature of the gas inside the cylinder?

(d) ... what is the pressure inside the cylinder?

(e) ... what is the average kinetic energy of every particle of gas in the container?

(f) ... what is the total momentum of the gas in the container?

(g) ... what is the net force on the inside walls of the container due to gas pressure?

B2. Imagine that the gas is cooled by bringing it into contact with ice–water. Which of the following quantities change as a result? For each quantity that changes, does it go up or down?

(a) pressure

(b) volume

(c) temperature

(d) average kinetic energy per particle

(e) number of gas particles inside the cylinder

(f) total momentum

(g) inner surface area

B3. Imagine now that someone pushes the piston down slowly with a force F exerted straight down on top of the piston. Which of the quantities in B2 above change as a result? For each quantity that changes, does it go up or down?

Reflection

R1. In part A, in which a single gas particle bounces back and forth inside a rigid box...

   (a) ... is work done on the gas particle during any time interval? When? Does the kinetic energy of the gas particle change as a result? Explain any contradictions.

   (b) ... is an impulse delivered to the gas particle during any time interval? When? Does the momentum of the gas particle change as a result? Explain any contradictions.

R2. In part B, in which a collection of N gas particles are inside a cylindrical container...

   (a) ... is work done by the gravitational force in situation B2? If so, is the work done positive or negative? What does the gravitational force do work on? What other forces do work? Where does the energy go? Does the total kinetic energy of the gas increase or decrease in B2? Explain any contradictions.

   (b) ... is work done by the external force F in situation B3? If so, is the work done positive or negative? What does the external force do work on? Where does the energy go? Does the total kinetic energy of the gas increase or decrease? Explain any contradictions.

R3. Is the pressure in situation B2 larger than, smaller than, or the same as the pressure in situation B3? Explain.

R4. What is the *specific heat* of a perfect gas? (That is, how much energy is needed to raise one gram of a perfect gas by one degree Kelvin?) What additional information do you need to determine the specific heat?

R5. (a) Sketch the temperature T vs. time t for situation B3. Label your sketch. Explain.

   (b) Sketch the total kinetic energy of the gas vs. time t. Label your sketch. In particular, when the kinetic energy is increasing, indicate where the energy comes from, and when the kinetic energy is decreasing, indicate where the energy goes.

Counting States in a Simple System

Purpose and Expected Outcome

This activity is the first in a series of activities designed to help you learn about *entropy* and its role in describing the *state* of a system. You will learn how to distinguish states from each other and learn how to identify the full range of states for a particular system.

Prior Experience / Knowledge Needed

No special prior experience is needed for this activity.

STATES OF A SYSTEM

The *state* of a system is a description of the system using characteristics that are different for one state than for another state. For example, when a coin is flipped, there are two states: heads up and tails up (or heads up and heads down). For one die, there are six states.

When there are two or more items in a system, each state can be described using the individual states of the components of the system. So, for instance, when two coins are flipped, there are 4 states of the system: two individual states (H or T) for each of the two coins. We can describe the four states as HH, HT, TH, and TT. When two dice are rolled, there are 36 possible states: six individual states for each of the two dice.

Explanation of Activity

There are two parts in this activity.

PART A: Identifying Possible States of a Simple System

List the possible individual states of a system of objects and use your list to answer questions about the different states of the system.

Example. Consider a system consisting of 2 coins. Let H represent heads and T tails. The coins are placed in a closed box that is vigorously shaken then opened.

(a) List all the possible states of the system.

(b) For what fraction of the states do both coins have the same orientation?

(c) For what fraction of the states are there an equal number of heads and tails?

Answer:

(a) *Possible states of 2 coins:*

State	Coin A	Coin B
1	H	H
2	H	T
3	T	H
4	T	T

(b) *Two of the four states have the coins in the same individual state (#'s 1 and 4), so the fraction is 1/2.*

(c) *Two of the four states have one head and one tail (#'s 2 and 3), so the fraction is 1/2.*

A1. Consider a system consisting of 3 coins. Let H represent heads and T tails. The coins are placed in a closed box that is vigorously shaken then opened.

(a) List all the possible states of the system.

(b) For what fraction of the states are all the coins facing heads up?

(c) For what fraction of the states do all the coins have the same orientation?

A2. Consider a system consisting of 4 coins. Let H represent heads and T tails. The coins are placed in a closed box that is vigorously shaken then opened.

(a) List all the possible states of the system. What is the total number of possible states?

(b) For what fraction of the states are all the coins facing heads up?

(c) For what fraction of the states do all the coins have the same orientation?

(d) For what fraction of the states is there an equal number of heads and tails?

(e) For what fraction of the states is there at least one head?

(f) For how many states are there no tails? no heads?

continued

A3. Consider a system consisting of 6 coins. The coins are placed in a closed box with each coin facing heads up. The box is vigorously shaken then opened.

   (a) For what fraction of the possible states of this system do all the coins have tails facing up?

   (b) What is the most likely number of heads? Explain.

   (c) The box is now closed again and shaken again, then opened. What is the most likely number of heads now?

   (d) For how many states are there no tails facing up? ... no heads facing up?

A4. Consider a system consisting of N coins. The coins are placed in a closed box that is vigorously shaken then opened.

   (a) How many possible states are there of N coins? Explain.

   (b) What is the most likely number of heads? Explain.

   (c) What is the least likely number of heads? Estimate its likelihood.

A5. Consider a system consisting of 2 dice. The dice are placed in a closed box that is vigorously shaken then opened.

   (a) List all the possible states of the system. What is the total number of possible states?

   (b) For what fraction of the states is the sum on the two dice equal to 8?

   (c) For what fraction of the states is the sum on the two dice less than 6?

   (d) For what fraction of the states are the two dice the same?

   (e) Which is larger, the fraction whose sum is equal to 3 or the fraction whose sum is equal to 11? Explain.

   (f) This process is repeated 10 times, and the sum of the two dice is recorded each time. How many times would you expect the sum to be equal to 7? Explain.

PART B: Counting States Consistent with a Constraint

Consider a closed box with a set of seven bowls rigidly fixed to its bottom and arranged symmetrically on both sides of the box as shown below. All questions refer to the possible ways that identical stones can be placed in the bowls so that the box balances about a pivot located directly above the center bowl.

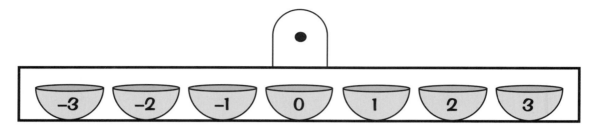

Example. Two stones of equal mass are placed in the box. One stone is blue, and the other is red.

(a) Assume first that the stones are distinguishable. List all the possible ways that the stones can be placed in the bowls and not violate the condition that the box balance on the pivot.

(b) How many distinguishable ways can the stones be placed in the bowls if we ignore their colors?

Answer:

(a) *The possibilities for two distinguishable stones are:*

State	Blue Stone	Red Stone
1	0	0
2	1	−1
3	−1	1
4	2	−2
5	−2	2
6	3	−3
7	−3	3

(b) *If the colors of the stones are ignored, there are only 4 possibilities:*

$$(0,0), (1,-1), (2,-2), \text{ and } (3,-3)$$

(If the numbers are different, either stone can be in either bowl. This means that there are still 7 different ways of putting the two stones in the bowls, but only 4 combinations are distinguishable from each other when we ignore the colors of the stones.)

continued

B1. Three distinguishable stones—one blue, one red, and one green—all having the same mass, are placed in the box.

(a) List all the possible ways that the stones can be placed in the bowls and not violate the condition that the box balance on the pivot.

(b) If we ignore their colors, how many distinguishable ways can three stones be placed in the bowls?

(c) For what fractions of the states would you find the green stone in each of the bowls? (For instance, for what fraction of the states would you find the green stone in the bowl labeled "0"? "1"? etc.) Are these fractions the same or different than the fractions for the blue stone? Explain.

B2. Four stones are placed in the box, and let n be the number of ways that two <u>identical</u> stones can be placed in the bowls.

(a) Assume first that the four stones are identical to each other. Is the number of ways that you can place four identical stones in the box greater than, less than, or equal to $2n$? Explain.

(b) Suppose now that two of the stones are identical to each other but slightly heavier than the other two which are also identical to each other. Is the number of ways that the four stones can be placed in the box greater than, less than, or equal to $2n$? If the number is not equal to $2n$, what is it equal to?

B3. Using all four of the situations examined so far—the example, B1, B2(a), and B2(b)—make a table showing, for each situation:

(a) the number of stones;

(b) a brief description of their masses;

(c) the number of ways <u>distinguishable</u> stones may be placed in the bowls and still keep the box balanced;

(d) the number of ways <u>identical</u> stones may be placed in the bowls and still keep the box balanced; and

(e) the <u>total</u> number of ways that identical stones may be placed in the bowls (without necessarily keeping the box balanced).

Reflection

R1. (a) How many possible states are there for three dice?

(b) For how many states is the total sum of the three dice equal to 9?

R2. Which is larger, the number of states possible when the components of a system are distinguishable, or the number when the components are identical? Explain. Is this <u>always</u> true, or only sometimes true?

R3. Which is larger, the number of states possible with 6 coins, or the number possible with 2 dice? Why are they different, even though there are 12 "sides" available in both systems?

R4. Suppose you had two dice shaped in the form of dodecahedrons (each consisting of 12 pentagons). The sides are labeled 1 through 12.

(a) How many states are possible for this system?

(b) For how many states is the total sum equal to 12?

(c) What is the most likely total sum?

(d) The dice are rolled 20 times. How many times do you expect the total sum to be equal to 12?

R5. Consider the box, bowls and stones in part B.

(a) For a system of 8 stones, how many total states are possible (without necessarily keeping the box balanced)?

(b) For a system of N stones, how many total states are possible (without necessarily keeping the box balanced)?

(c) For a system of N stones and M bowls, how many total states are possible (without necessarily keeping the box balanced)?

R6. Create and describe a system in which the total number of possible states is 15.

R7. Create and describe a system of two dice in which the total number of possible states is 16.

Exploring Equilibrium
in a Complex System

Purpose and Expected Outcome

This activity is the second leading up to the idea of *entropy* and its role in describing the state of a system. In this activity you will learn how to identify states in a complex system, and how this is different than identifying states in a simple system. You will also learn about *equilibrium* as applied to complex systems and how to recognize when a system has reached equilibrium and when a system is not in equilibrium.

Prior Experience / Knowledge Needed

No special prior experience is needed for this activity. Some experience with simple systems is desirable, such as systems of a few coins or two dice.

IDENTIFYING STATES IN A COMPLEX SYSTEM

In small simple systems, such as those consisting of a few coins or a couple of dice, it is relatively easy to identify states by recording the individual states of the components of the system. For instance, there are four states of two coins: HH, HT, TH, and TT. These are sometimes called *microstates* of the system. When the number of coins gets too large, it is inconvenient and often unimportant to label system states according to individual states. States in a complex system are usually labeled by the <u>number</u> of components in a particular state. For example, a system of 10 coins has only 11 *macrostates*: H^{10}, H^9T, H^8T^2, ... , HT^9, T^{10}, where the exponent refers to the number of heads or tails in the state. Each macrostate (except H^{10} and T^{10}) can be made from many different microstates, depending on which individual coins are heads and which are tails. For example, H^9T can be made from 10 different microstates of the system.

Explanation of Activity

There are two systems to study in this activity.

SYSTEM A: One Hundred Pennies in a Shallow Box

Assume you have 100 pennies in a box that is so shallow that when the box is shaken up-and-down once, at most only a few coins flip. Initially all of the coins are heads up.

A1.   Estimate the dimensions of the box. Explain your estimate.

A2.   (a)   After one shake, list the possible macrostates of the system.

      (b)   After two shakes, list the possible macrostates of the system.

A3.   Sketch the number of heads facing up as a function of the number of times the box is shaken.

A second box of 100 pennies is prepared with 50 coins heads up and the rest tails up. This box is labeled 50H. The first box is labeled 100H because initially all 100 coins are facing heads up.

A4.   After one shake...

      (a)   ... which box <u>might</u> have a different number of heads facing up? Explain.

      (b)   ... which box <u>is more likely</u> to have a different number of heads facing up? Explain.

A5.   After 500 shakes...

      (a)   ... which box <u>might</u> have a different number of heads facing up than it did without any shakes? (In other words, which box might have changed macrostates?) Explain.

      (b)   ... which box is more likely to have a different number of heads facing up than it did without any shakes? (In other words, which box is more likely to have changed macrostates?) Explain.

      (c)   ... which box do you expect to change more than the other? How did it change? Explain. How much did the other box change? Explain.

A6.   Are either of these systems in equilibrium at the beginning (before any shaking)? Explain. (In particular, explain what is meant by the term *equilibrium* in this context.)

A7.   What is the equilibrium macrostate of 200 coins in a box?

EQUILIBRIUM

The term *equilibrium* is often used to indicate that some characteristic of an object or system does not change with time. Its use depends critically on what you keep track of and what you ignore. For instance, we say that a ball rolling with constant speed is in *dynamic* equilibrium, because the net force on it is zero, so its velocity is not changing, even though its position is changing. A gas is said to be in *thermal* equilibrium when the temperature of the gas is constant, which means also that the total energy of the system is constant, even though the kinetic energies of individual gas particles are constantly changing. So, when a complex system is in equilibrium, the macrostate of the system remains the same, even though the states of its components might change. In other words, in a system of coins, the numbers of heads and tails showing remains about the same, even though individual coins may flip from one side to the other. In fact, an equal number of coins must flip each way for the system to be in equilibrium.

SYSTEM B: Ninety Dice in a Shallow Box

Assume you have 90 dice in a box that is so shallow that when the box is shaken up-and-down once, at most only one or two dice change face. Initially all of the dice are showing one dot on its upper surface.

B1. How many different microstates are possible for the initial macrostate of the system? Explain.

B2. (a) After one shake, one die changes its face. How many different macrostates are possible now for the system? Explain.

    (b) After a second shake, a different die changes its face. How many different macrostates are possible now for the system? Explain.

B3. (a) Sketch the number of possible microstates as a function of the number of shakes.

    (b) What happens to the number of microstates as the number of shakes increases? Does this trend continue forever, or does it change at some time? Explain.

B4. Which is easier, to increase or to decrease the number of possible microstates in this system? Explain. Describe a method for doing each.

B5. Describe what equilibrium would look like for this system. Explain.

B6. At equilibrium, does shaking change the macrostate? Explain. Does shaking change the microstate? Explain.

Reflection

R1. (a) Is it appropriate to call the H^3T^3 state of a six-coin system an equilibrium state? Explain.

    (b) Is it appropriate to call the HHTHTT state of a six-coin system an equilibrium state? Explain.

R2. In B2(a), for each possible macrostate of the system, how many microstates are there? Describe them.

R3. (a) How many macrostates are possible for a six-coin system? a 100-coin system? a 200-coin system? a 1000-coin system?

    (b) How many microstates are possible for a six-coin system? a 100-coin system? a 200-coin system? a 1000-coin system?

R4. (a) Which macrostate(s) of the six-coin system has the largest number of microstates associated with it? Explain why you think so.

    (b) Which macrostate(s) of the six-coin system has the smallest number of microstates associated with it? Explain why you think so.

    (c) Which macrostate(s) of the 1000-coin system has the largest number of microstates associated with it? Explain why you think so.

    (d) Which macrostate(s) of the 1000-coin system is <u>farthest</u> from equilibrium? Explain.

R5. Explain why a system that is <u>not</u> in equilibrium will tend toward equilibrium when it is shaken.

R6. Interpret the following statement:

The most likely macrostate is the state we know least about.

CS·20

Exploring Entropy in a Complex System

Purpose and Expected Outcome

This activity is the third leading up to the idea of *entropy* and its role in describing the state of a system. In this activity you will learn how to associate the number of microstates in a system with your <u>lack</u> of knowledge of the system. Also, you will learn about the concept of *entropy*.

Prior Experience / Knowledge Needed

You should know the difference between a *microstate* and a *macrostate* of a system. You should be able to recognize when a system has reached *equilibrium*. You should have some experience labeling and counting states of a system.

Explanation of Activity

There are two systems to study in this activity.

SYSTEM A: Four Pennies in a Shallow Box

Assume you have 4 pennies. In each of the following questions, label microstates using the individual states of each coin. For instance, THTT means that the 2nd coin is heads up and the rest are tails up. Label macrostates according to how many coins are heads up and how many are tails up. For instance, HT^3 means that there is only one coin heads up and the rest are tails up.

A1. List all the possible microstates of the system. How many possible microstates are there?

A2. List all the possible macrostates of the system. How many possible macrostates are there?

A3. Make a table showing:
- (a) the possible macrostates of the system;
- (b) for each macrostate, the possible microstates of the system consistent with that macrostate; and
- (c) for each macrostate, the number of possible microstates of the system.

A4. (a) Which macrostate(s) has the smallest number of microstates associated with it?
(b) Which macrostate(s) has the largest number of microstates associated with it?

A5. The 4 pennies are put into a box that is so shallow that when the box is shaken, at most one or two pennies change their states.
- (a) Which macrostate(s) is farthest from equilibrium? Explain.
- (b) Which macrostate(s) is closest to equilibrium? Explain.
- (c) Which macrostate(s) do you know least about? Explain.
- (d) Which macrostate(s) do you know most about? Explain.

Knowing some property of a complex system may not tell us anything about the individual components of the system. For instance, if you know that a system of 4 coins is in the 4-head (H^4) state you know the state of every individual coin in the system, because there is only one way of arranging the coins (HHHH). However, if you are told that there are 2 heads and 2 tails, all you know is that the system can be in any one of 6 microstates (HHTT, HTTH, HTHT, etc.). Viewed another way, if you are told, for instance, that there are 2 heads and 2 tails, you know nothing about the state of any particular coin. This is because in 3 of the 6 possible microstates that particular coin is in the head state while in the other 3 it is in the tail state.

The "headness" of a system of 4 coins has 5 possible values: 0H, 1H, 2H, 3H, and 4H. This "headness" is analogous to a macroscopic quantity, such as volume or temperature. The 2H-state (H^2T^2) has the largest number of microstates consistent with it (6). A new thermodynamic quantity called *entropy* is defined to be a measure of the number of microstates associated with a particular macrostate. As the number of microstates increases, so does the entropy. Therefore, the 2H-state has the largest entropy, because it has the largest number of microstates associated with it.

We can now characterize the *thermodynamic* equilibrium state of a complex system. (This is different but similar to *thermal* equilibrium.) The thermodynamic equilibrium state of a complex system is the state of maximum entropy. If we assume that all microstates of the system are equally likely, then (for instance) the 2H-state is the most likely and therefore the equilibrium state. This state has the maximum number of microstates (6) consistent with its macroscopic quantities (2H)

Because our knowledge of the state of any individual component decreases as the entropy increases, entropy is sometimes referred to as the lack of information about the components of a complex system. For example, the 0H and 4H states contain no lack of information about the states of the individual coins, because there is only 1 way to arrange the coins in each of these states, so these states have zero entropy.

PART B: Relating Equilibrium and Entropy

Consider a system similar to that described in Activity CS·18 (*Counting States in a Simple System*), part B, in which a small number of stones was distributed among 7 bowls in a box. Assume now there are 25 bowls and 600 stones in the box. The bowls and the box have negligible mass compared to the stones. Assume also that the stones may be in any bowl. To identify the macrostate of the box, we measure its balance point.

Initially all the stones start in the bowl at the extreme left-hand side of the box, and with each shake of the box, at most one or two stones move at most one bowl to the left or right. Keep in mind that *equilibrium* in this context means *thermodynamic* equilibrium.

B1. With the box in the initial configuration...
    (a) ... where does the box balance?
    (b) ... how many microstates are associated with the initial macrostate?
    (c) ... what is your <u>lack</u> of knowledge of the microstates of the system?
    (d) ... what is the entropy of the system?

B2. After one shake, how many macrostates of the box are possible? What are they?

B3. After only a few shakes, where would you expect the box to balance?

B4. (a) After 1000 shakes, where would you expect the box to balance? Explain.
    (b) At equilibrium, where would you expect the box to balance? Explain.

B5. After a very large number of shakes, how many stones would you expect to be in each bowl?

B6. Sketch the entropy of the system as a function of the number of shakes.

B7. Suppose now that the box is in a macrostate with 24 bowls equally filled and the middle bowl is empty.
    (a) Is the system in equilibrium? Explain.
    (b) Is the system at maximum entropy? Explain.
    (c) Describe what happens to the microstates and to the entropy of the system when the box is shaken many times.
    (d) What is the <u>least</u> number of shakes needed to bring the box into equilibrium?

B8. Suppose now there are 1200 stones in the left-most bowl. Do you think it would take more or fewer shakes for the system to reach its equilibrium balance point? Explain.

Reflection

R1. Which is larger, the number of microstates or the number of macrostates in a system? Explain. Is this always true, or only sometimes true?

R2. Reconsider your answers to part A. Is the sum of the values in column (c) of your table in A3 equal to your answer to A1? Why or why not? Did you check your answers to A3 when you were filling out the table to make sure they were consistent with A1 and A2? Why or why not?

R3. Explain why the most likely macrostate of a system has the greatest lack of knowledge about it.

R4. Explain for a multi-coin system that is <u>not</u> in equilibrium why it is very likely that the system, when it is shaken, will tend toward the equilibrium state.

R5. Explain why for a multi-coin system in equilibrium it is very likely that the system, if it is shaken, is not likely to go very far from equilibrium.

R6. Entropy is sometimes said to be a measure of *randomness* or *disorder*. Entropy is maximum for equilibrium states. For an equilibrium state, what is it that is "random" or "disordered"?

CS·21

Relating Entropy to Realistic Systems

Purpose and Expected Outcome

In this activity you will apply the concept of *entropy* to realistic thermodynamic systems where each microstate is determined by the individual states of atoms or molecules. After completing this activity you will be able to use the concept of *entropy* to analyze and reason about a variety of situations.

Prior Experience / Knowledge Needed

You should have some experience with simple systems such as a few coins or a couple of dice and with complex systems such as hundreds of coins or dice. You should know the difference between a *microstate* and a *macrostate* of a system. You should have some experience with the idea of *thermodynamic equilibrium*, and you should know what is meant by *entropy* in the most general sense.

"REAL" THERMODYNAMIC SYSTEMS

The complex systems you have been working with are not actually *thermodynamic* systems, in part because they are artificial and not as complicated as actual thermodynamic systems, such as a box of gas. Even when the number of coins in a system is 1000 or even 10,000, we can still imagine counting the macrostates or listing the microstates of the system. It is much, much more difficult to deal with the microstates of a gas, which depend on the positions and kinetic energies of every gas particle. (A typical thermodynamic system has about 10^{23} particles in it!)

continued

When you are struggling to understand "real" thermodynamic systems, it will help to think about these other systems and how quantities are related to each other. Often there is no need to count microstates, but rather only to understand how the number of states will change in response to a macroscopic change in the system, such as an increase in temperature or a decrease in volume. When analyzing these more complicated situations, we recommend you first consider a very small number of particles to see how changes in macroscopic quantities affect the number of microstates available. Keep in mind the notion that *entropy* is a measure of information—the less we know about the actual microstate of the system, the higher the entropy.

Explanation of Activity

There are two parts in this activity.

PART A: Comparing Entropy Under Different Conditions

A1. Consider the five systems shown below, each consisting of a box of ideal gas. Assume the size of the box is proportional to its volume, and the number of black dots is proportional to the total number of gas particles. The temperature in each box is shown. System E is at temperature $2T$. System F consists of two separate boxes.

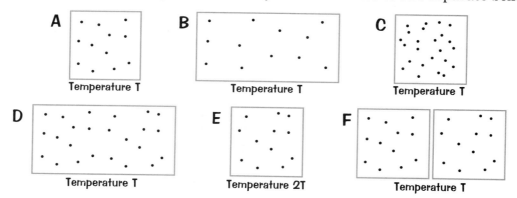

Which system has the larger entropy...

(a) ... A or B? Explain.

(b) ... A or C? Explain.

(c) ... A or D? Explain.

(d) ... A or E? Explain.

(e) ... A or F? Explain.

(f) ... D or F? Explain.

continued

A2. Compare the entropies for the following ideal gas systems, which all have the same total kinetic energy E and volume V, and all have the same number of particles N.

   F: The particles have a distribution of kinetic energy values ranging from zero up to several times E/N.

   G: Half of the particles have kinetic energy E/N, while the rest have a distribution of kinetic energies.

   H: All particles have exactly the same kinetic energy E/N.

   I: Half of the particles have zero kinetic energy, while the rest have a distribution of kinetic energies.

   J: One particle has kinetic energy E, while the rest have zero kinetic energy.

Put these five systems in order from smallest to largest entropy, and explain your answer.

A3. Two systems are prepared identically (i.e., same pressure, temperature, and volume) with equal amounts of the same gas. In one (A), the piston is held fixed. In the other (B), the gas is compressed by slowly pushing on the piston and then the piston is held fixed. Both systems are thermally insulated from the environment.

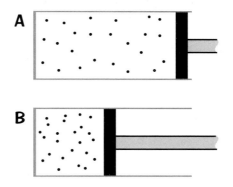

   (a) Which system, A or B, has more energy in it? Explain.

   (b) Which system, A or B, has the higher temperature? Explain.

   (c) Which system, A or B, has the larger entropy? Explain.

A4. Consider two similarly prepared containers of gas, one carried in a car traveling at 50mi/h, while the other is on a train traveling at 100mi/h.

   (a) Which gas has the larger energy? Explain.

   (b) Which gas has the larger temperature? Explain.

   (c) Which gas has the larger entropy? Explain.

PART B: Identifying Changes in Entropy

B1. For each of the following processes, if possible, determine whether the entropy increases, decreases, or stays the same. Be prepared to explain your answers.

(a) A gas within a small, thermally insulated canister is allowed to expand into a large, evacuated (and thermally insulated) box.

(b) Heat is added to a chunk of metal.

(c) A half empty bottle of soda is shaken.

(d) A block slides across a table eventually coming to rest.

B2. A small piece of metal at 0°C is placed in a large pot of hot water at 100°C. After a long time the piece of metal is removed from the pot and placed in a tub of ice–water mixture at 0°C. The following questions refer to the time interval when the metal first touches the ice–water mixture until it comes to equilibrium in the ice–water bath.

(a) The total change in entropy of the piece of metal is:

      (A) positive.   (B) negative.   (C) zero.   (D) Its change cannot be determined.

(b) The total change in entropy of the hot water is:

      (A) positive.   (B) negative.   (C) zero.   (D) Its change cannot be determined.

(c) The total change in entropy of the ice–water bath is:

      (A) positive.   (B) negative.   (C) zero.   (D) Its change cannot be determined.

(d) Compare the magnitude of the entropy change for the piece of metal, the boiling water, and the ice–water mixture.

(e) The total change in entropy for the entire system is:

      (A) positive.   (B) negative.   (C) zero.   (D) Its change cannot be determined.

B3. A glass of hot water is mixed with a glass of cold water. Does entropy increase, decrease or stay the same or can the change in entropy not be determined? Explain your answer.

B4. A box is made with a removable wall that divides the box into equal halves as shown. The left side is filled with a gas at temperature T until the pressure is P. The right side is filled with a different gas at temperature T until it also reaches pressure P. At a certain time, the wall is removed.

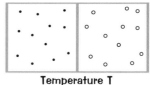
Temperature T

(a) What are the final temperature and pressure of the mixture? Explain.

(b) The change in entropy of the system is:

      (A) positive.   (B) negative.   (C) zero.   (D) Its change cannot be determined.

Reflection and Integration of Ideas

R1. Consider a system consisting of one particle of gas in a box.

    (a) Is the entropy of the system zero or non-zero? Explain.

    (b) Would the entropy change if the box were bigger? How?

    (c) Which is more likely, that the particle is in one corner of the box or that it is in the center of the box?

R2. Consider a system consisting of two particles of gas in a box. One particle has energy E and the other has energy $2E$. The two particles interact <u>only</u> through elastic collisions.

    (a) Do you expect the entropy to increase, decrease, or stay the same as a function of time? Explain.

    (b) After a very long time, is it possible for the energy of one of the particles to be equal to E? How likely do you suppose it is? Explain. Which particle is more likely to have energy E?

    (c) After a very long time, which is more likely, that one of the particles has energy E or that it has energy $3/2E$? Explain.

R3. (a) How would your answers to B4 change if the gases in the two halves of the box were identical? Explain.

    (b) What if the wall is now replaced in the middle of the box? What would happen to the entropy of the system?

    (c) What would happen to the entropy of the system if one half contained a gas at temperature T, and the other half contained the same gas at temperature $2T$ before the wall is removed? Would the entropy increase, decrease, or stay the same?

R4. All other factors remaining the same...

    (a) ... how does the entropy of a system change when the volume is increased? Explain.

    (b) ... how does the entropy of a system change when the temperature is increased? Explain.

    (c) ... how does the entropy of a system change when the *phase* changes, such as when a solid melts or when a liquid evaporates? Explain.

R5. (a) What happens to the volume of ice when it melts into liquid water? Does it increase or decrease? What implications might this feature have on the change in entropy of the ice when it melts?

    (b) Which of the following molecules of H_2O has more locations available to it, a molecule within the liquid phase or a molecule in the solid phase? Explain. What implications might this feature have on the change in entropy of the ice when it melts?

Reasoning Using Entropy Ideas

Purpose and Expected Outcome

In this activity you will use the idea of *entropy* to analyze and reason about a variety of situations.

Prior Experience / Knowledge Needed

You should have some experience with simple systems such as a few coins or a couple of dice and with complex systems such as hundreds of coins or dice. You should know the difference between a *microstate* and a *macrostate* of a system. You should have some experience with the idea of *thermodynamic equilibrium*, and you should know what is meant by *entropy* in the most general sense. Finally, you should be familiar with the Perfect Gas Law ($PV = nRT_K$).

Explanation of Activity

There are four situations to consider in this activity.

SITUATION A

An ideal gas is put into a container as shown below. The container has a piston at one end and a wall that may be removed through the side of the container without losing any gas. The gas is thermally isolated from its environment.

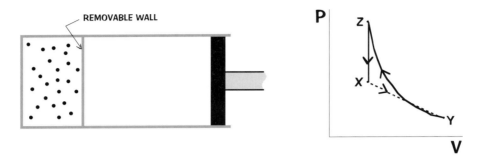

The gas is taken around the cycle shown above to the right. Initially, in state X, the gas is confined by the wall to $1/3$ of its maximum volume. The wall is then removed, which allows the gas to expand to 3 times its initial volume, as shown by the dashed line from state X to state Y. (The dashed line is used to indicate that the gas is not in equilibrium during this expansion, and so, the pressure and volume cannot be defined until the expansion is complete.) Next, the wall is replaced just inside the piston, and the gas is compressed along the curved line to its original volume (state Z in the diagram). The wall is held fixed, but the piston is returned to its initial position. Finally, the pressure is lowered at constant volume to its original pressure by removing some energy from the gas, as shown by the solid line connecting states Z and X.

A1. Make three drawings, one for each of the three states, X, Y, and Z, showing the location of the wall, the gas, and the piston when the system is in that state.

A2. (a) Which state(s) has the largest temperature? Explain.
     (b) Which state(s) has the smallest temperature? Explain.

A3. (a) During which process(es) is the entropy increasing? Explain.
     (b) During which process(es) is the entropy decreasing? Explain.
     (c) Are there any processes for which you cannot determine whether the entropy is increasing or decreasing? Why not?

A4. What is the change in entropy for the gas as it completes one cycle? (In other words, what is the overall change in entropy as the gas goes from X to Y to Z and back to X again?) Explain.

SITUATION B

A canister of air is at a pressure P slightly greater than the air pressure in a room (P_0). Both the canister and the room are at temperature T. A valve is opened so that some air escapes from the canister. When air stops leaving the canister, the valve is closed again.

B1. Does the entropy of the air in the canister change? What assumptions have you made to answer this question?

Many days later, the air pressure in the room has increased. The temperature is still T. The valve on the canister is reopened and air flows back into the canister until it contains the same amount of air it did originally.

B2. What is the air pressure in the room? What is the final air pressure in the canister? Explain.

B3. Does the entropy of the air in the canister change? Explain.

B4. What is the overall change in the entropy of the air in the canister from before the original canister is opened until after the valve is reopened three days later? Explain.

SITUATION C

Consider a glass containing ice (solid H_2O) and water (liquid H_2O) in thermal equilibrium at $0°C$. (At equilibrium the amount of ice—and therefore also the amount of water—remains constant.) However, if the surrounding environment is at a temperature greater than $0°C$ the ice will melt, but as long as there is ice in the water, both the ice and the water remain at $0°C$ (assuming that the ice and water stay thoroughly mixed).

C1. (a) Sketch the temperature of the ice–water mixture as a function of time.
   (b) Sketch the energy of the ice–water mixture as a function of time.
   (c) Sketch the volume of the ice–water mixture as a function of time.

C2. When ice melts in water at $0°C$, the total volume of H_2O:

   (A) increases.   (B) decreases.   (C) stays the same.   (D) Its change cannot be determined.

C3. As the ice changes to water, the total energy of the ice–water mixture:

   (A) increases.   (B) decreases.   (C) stays the same.   (D) Its change cannot be determined.

C4. As the ice changes to water, the total entropy of the ice–water mixture:

   (A) increases.   (B) decreases.   (C) stays the same.   (D) Its change cannot be determined.

SITUATION D

An ideal gas is put into a container as shown below. The container has a piston at one

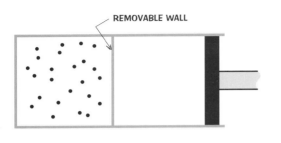

REMOVABLE WALL

end and a wall that may be removed through the side of the container without losing any gas. The gas is thermally isolated from its environment.

In step 1, the wall is removed, allowing the gas to fill the whole compartment, doubling the volume of the gas. In step 2, the wall is replaced just inside the piston (as shown in state X of situation A) and the gas is slowly compressed until it reaches its original volume. In step 3, the wall is secured, and the piston is returned to its original position. This sequence is repeated 4 more times.

D1.   Sketch the pressure P vs. the volume V for this entire process.

D2.   Sketch temperature T vs. time t. Label your sketch according to what is being done to the gas during each time interval.

D3.   (a)   During which step(s) is the entropy increasing? Explain. Decreasing? Explain.

   (b)   Are there any steps for which you cannot determine whether the entropy is increasing or decreasing? Why not?

Summary

Entropy is an example of a *state function*, which means that whenever a system in a particular state (e.g., P, V, and T) returns to its original state, the entropy is also the same as it was originally. So, in situation A, the overall change in entropy of the gas is zero when it returns to state X. Also, in situation B, the overall change in entropy of the gas in the canister is zero, because it has also returned to its original state.

Situation D is different. Each time the gas is compressed, its energy and temperature increase. But each time the gas expands to fill the entire container, its energy and temperature stay the same. So even though the volume of the gas returns to its original value, the pressure and the temperature are different. This means that the state is different, and so the entropy is different also. In fact, because the temperature is higher, the total energy is higher, so there are more microstates available to the gas particles and the entropy is higher also.

In situation C, the *phase* of matter (solid, liquid, or gas) also affects the state. When ice melts, even though the volume is decreasing, the available locations of each H_2O molecule are increasing, so the entropy of the ice–water mixture is increasing also.

Reflection

R1. Is *temperature* a *state function*? Explain. If a certain amount of gas is brought back to its original pressure and volume, will it always return to its original temperature? Explain why or why not. If not, describe a process or circumstance in which the gas has a different temperature, even though it has its original pressure and volume. What other quantities are state functions?

R2. Reconsider situation A, in which an ideal gas is taken around a cycle using a removable wall and a piston. Assume that initially, in state X, the temperature of the gas is T.

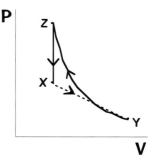

First, the wall is removed, allowing the gas to expand to fill the container (dashed line in the diagram).

   (a) Does the energy of the gas change? Explain why or why not. If so, where does the energy come from (or where does it go)?

   (b) Does the temperature of the gas change? Explain why or why not.

Next, the gas is compressed to its original volume, but its pressure is much higher than it was originally (state Z in the diagram).

   (c) Does the energy of the gas change? Explain why or why not. If so, where does the energy come from (or where does it go)?

   (d) Does the temperature of the gas change? Explain why or why not.

Finally, energy is removed from the gas, bringing it back to its original pressure.

   (e) Does the temperature of the gas change? Why do you think so?

   (f) How does the temperature of the gas compare to the original temperature T? Explain.

R3. Reconsider situation B, in which a canister of air loses a small amount of gas and then later gains back the same amount of air.

   (a) What exactly is meant by the "amount" of air?

   (b) When the pressure in the room has increased, what <u>must</u> be true about the "amount" of air in the room? Explain your answer.

R4. When you add energy to a <u>closed</u> system, the entropy of the system:

     (A) increases.   (B) decreases.   (C) stays the same.   (D) Its change depends on the situation.

Explain your answer, and give examples to illustrate. (**Hint:** There are only two ways to add energy to a closed system: by doing work and by heat flow. Consider different phases of matter and consider phases in equilibrium, such as ice and water at 0°C.)

Reasoning and Problem Solving in Complex Systems

Purpose and Expected Outcome

In this activity you will apply the ideas you have learned about pressure, temperature, heat, volume, and entropy to a variety of situations.

Prior Experience / Knowledge Needed

The problem situations in this activity are not simple. You may need additional information or have to learn about new concepts to fully complete what you are asked to do. You will need to interact with your teacher and consult reference books. For each problem make sure you have a good understanding of the situation by discussing the problem with your teacher and classmates. Describe any relationships you know exist. Try to develop a plan or strategy for solving the problem. Think about experiences that may relate to similar situations in the problems. It is more important for you to formulate and express your ideas than worry about being right.

Explanation of Activity

There are 9 problems to consider in this activity. Keep in mind that you may not have enough information and/or knowledge to finish each problem without supplementing what you know.

A1. A block of metal at room temperature (26°C) is put into an insulated beaker containing 940cm³ of water at 10°C. With the block of metal in the water, the waterline on the beaker is at 1040cm³. The equilibrium temperature of the water and metal is 18°C. If the piece of metal is a pure element, what element is it most likely to be?

A2. On an otherwise calm day you can have gentle breezes near the ocean shore. The pattern of the breezes in the summer at a certain location is such that the breeze blows toward the shore during the heat of the day and toward the ocean during the evening.

(a) What mechanisms could be responsible for this phenomenon?

(b) Explain why the breeze is on shore during the day and off shore at night.

(c) What do you think happens to this pattern of breezes during the winter?

A3. During cycles of global warming the polar ice caps can begin to melt, decreasing the total amount of ice present.

(a) Estimate how much energy it would take to melt the polar ice caps.

(b) Compare this with how much energy it would take to boil away the oceans.

(c) How many hours/days/years would it take for the Earth to absorb enough energy from the sun to melt the polar ice caps?

A4. Machines provide mechanical advantage by amplifying the force one can exert on an object. Levers, inclines, and pulleys are examples of simple machines that provide mechanical advantage. Nevertheless simple machines never provide advantage when it comes to doing work. For example, the minimal amount of energy needed to lift an object is the same whether we use a simple machine or not.

(a) The work done by a simple machine must always be less than or equal to the energy put into operating the machine. Explain why. Identify any assumptions.

(b) Give some examples of how simple machines can be used to do work.

(c) For each example identify the factors that contribute to inefficiencies in using the input energy to do work.

(d) Is there any theoretical limit to how efficient a simple machine can be. Could you make the machine as efficient as desired? Illustrate your answer with an example.

continued

A5. Machines that use heat transfer to gain energy to do work are called *heat engines*. A very simple example of a heat engine is shown in the diagram at right. A cylindrical container is closed except for two tubes angled as shown. When water in the container starts to boil, steam emerges from the tubes on the sides, causing the container to spin. If the container is attached to an axle it can do work on the surrounding environment.

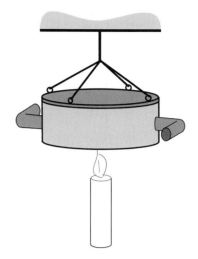

(a) After the water starts to boil how will the amount of work done compare to the thermal energy transferred to the container? (Is the work less than, more than, or the same as the transferred thermal energy, or is the comparison not possible?) Explain.

(b) Can a heat engine be used to gain an energy advantage, that is, can a heat engine do more work than the amount of energy put into the machine?

(c) What factors contribute to the effectiveness of using thermal energy to do work? How might you improve the efficiency of this heat engine to do work?

(d) Is there any theoretical limit as to how much work you can get from this machine per amount of thermal energy? If so, provide specific information about the limiting factors.

A6. The temperature of a lake in a region with a changeable climate can vary significantly throughout the year. While the lake is warming up or cooling down the temperature can vary with depth. For example, on a warm summer day the water in a deep lake will seem noticeably colder at greater depths.

(a) What processes contribute to the temperature variation with depth in lake water?

(b) In your estimation, which process(es) have the greatest impact on temperature variation with depth?

(c) Do you think the temperature variation with depth would be greater when the air temperature is 10°C above the average lake temperature or when it is 10°C below the average lake temperature? Explain.

A7. During the winter ice forms at the surface of a lake.

(a) What processes contribute to this phenomenon?

(b) If the air temperature remained constant would the <u>rate</u> of freezing increase, decrease, or stay the same as time went on? Explain.

continued

A8. A canister with $2^1/_2$ moles of O_2 gas has a movable piston and platform at one end (shown in black). The surface areas of the top of the block, the top of the platform, and the bottom of the canister are shown also. The initial height h of the bottom of the piston is 1m.

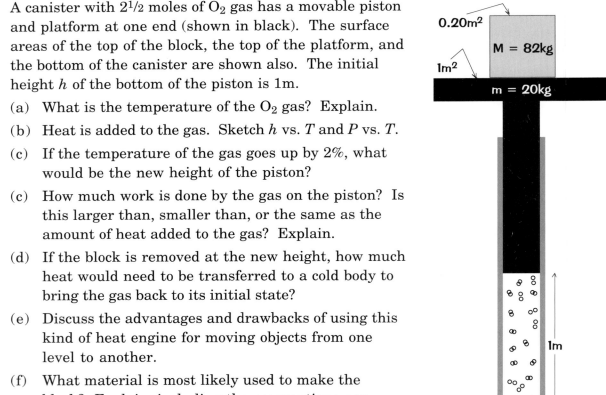

(a) What is the temperature of the O_2 gas? Explain.

(b) Heat is added to the gas. Sketch h vs. T and P vs. T.

(c) If the temperature of the gas goes up by 2%, what would be the new height of the piston?

(c) How much work is done by the gas on the piston? Is this larger than, smaller than, or the same as the amount of heat added to the gas? Explain.

(d) If the block is removed at the new height, how much heat would need to be transferred to a cold body to bring the gas back to its initial state?

(e) Discuss the advantages and drawbacks of using this kind of heat engine for moving objects from one level to another.

(f) What material is most likely used to make the block? Explain, including the assumptions you made.

A9. For the previous problem situation, if the temperature of the gas is changed, the gas will expand or contract. If forces are applied to the gas, the gas will expand or contract. Solids and liquids will also expand or contract if their temperature is changed or they are subjected to forces.

(a) Explain why this occurs.

(b) If the temperature increases will the fluid/solid expand or contract.

(c) Ice at 0°C is put into a glass of water at 25°C so that the water line is at the rim. Is there any risk that the glass will overflow when the ice melts? Explain.

Reflection

R1. What drawings or graphs did you use to solve these problems? How did these help?

R2. Were you able to determine what you needed to know to solve each problem? What methods were most effective for determining what you did not know?

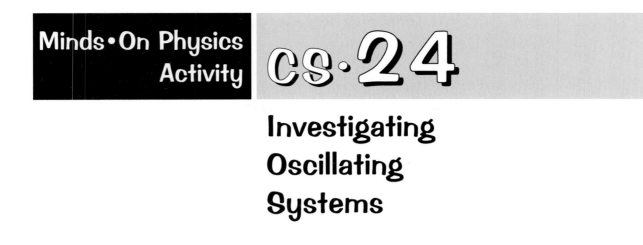

Investigating Oscillating Systems

Purpose and Expected Outcome

In this activity you will investigate the behavior of a few different systems that *oscillate*. You will apply the concepts and principles of Newtonian mechanics to determine why these systems oscillate and why they are periodic. After completing the activity you will be able to recognize the circumstances that lead to oscillatory motion.

Prior Experience / Knowledge Needed

You should be familiar with the spring force, local gravitation, and Newton's laws of motion. The idea of an equilibrium position or balance point—the position at which all the forces on an object balance—is also needed.

Explanation of Activity

There are two parts in this activity. In the first part, you will apply force ideas to oscillating systems. In the second part, you will apply energy ideas to them.

PART A: Analyzing Forces in Oscillating Systems

Answer the following questions about the forces on objects in oscillating systems.

A1. A cart is connected to a horizontal spring as shown. (Assume the cart rolls without slipping.) Assume that initially the spring is not stretched and the cart is not moving.

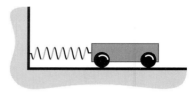

(a) If the cart is moved to the right and released is there a net force on the cart? If so, in what direction?

(b) If the cart is moved to the left and released, is there a net force on the cart? If so, in what direction?

(c) Sketch the net force on the cart as a function of <u>position</u> for the case where the cart is moved to the right and released.

(d) Sketch the net force on the cart as a function of <u>time</u> for the case where the cart is moved to the right and released.

A2. A block is connected to a vertical spring as shown. Assume that the block as shown does not move when released.

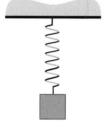

(a) Draw a free-body diagram for each of the following cases:

    i. The block is displaced a small distance upward.

    ii. The block is displaced a large distance upward.

    iii. The block is displaced a small distance downward.

    iv. The block is displaced a large distance downward.

(b) How is the direction of the net force on the block related to the direction of the displacement? Is it in the same direction, opposite direction, or does the direction depend upon the size of the displacement? Explain your answer.

(c) Sketch the net force on the block as a function of position.

A3. A ball is suspended from the ceiling using a short piece of light string. The ball is displaced to the right and released from position 1.

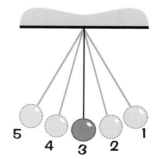

(a) Is the net force on the ball ever zero? If so, where?

(b) For each position indicate the direction of the acceleration of the ball.

(c) For positions 2 and 4, draw a free-body diagram for the ball.

(d) When is the tension in the string the greatest?

(e) Sketch the *x*- and *y*-components of the net force on the ball as functions of position.

PART B: Analyzing Energy in Oscillating Systems

Answer the following questions about the energy in oscillating systems.

B1. A cart is connected to a horizontal spring as shown. Assume the cart rolls without slipping. Assume also that the cart has been given a shove toward the right and is oscillating back and forth.

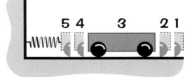

(a) At which position(s) will the cart's kinetic energy be the greatest? Explain.

(b) At which position(s) will the potential energy of the cart–spring system be the greatest? Explain.

(c) Compare the cart's speed at its equilibrium position traveling to the right with the cart's speed at its equilibrium position traveling to the left. Is the speed greater going right, greater going left, the same, or can it not be determined? Explain.

(d) For a cart that is pushed to the right, how will its maximum displacement to the right (as measured from the equilibrium position) compare with its maximum displacement to the left (as measured from the equilibrium position)? Is the maximum displacement greater to the right, to the left, or are they the same?

(e) Does the amount of time it takes for the cart to complete one cycle increase with time, decrease with time, or stay the same? Explain.

B2. A block is connected to a vertical spring as shown. Assume that the block has been given a shove downward from the equilibrium position and is oscillating up and down.

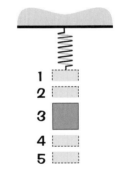

(a) At which position(s) is the gravitational potential energy maximum?

(b) At which position(s) is the spring potential energy maximum?

(c) At which position(s) is the kinetic energy maximum?

(d) For the equilibrium point compare the speed of the block traveling upward with the speed of the block traveling downward.

(e) Compare the maximum displacement up (as measured relative to the equilibrium position) with the maximum displacement down (also as measured relative to the equilibrium position).

(f) Compare the amount of time needed to go from the equilibrium position to the highest point with the amount of time needed to go from the equilibrium position to the lowest point.

continued

B3. A ball is connected to the end of a suspended string to form a pendulum. The ball is displaced to the right and released from rest at point 1.

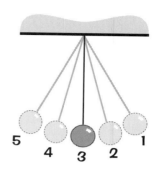

(a) Of the forces on the ball, which do work on it as it moves from point 1 to point 3?

(b) If the mass of the ball is changed, how will this affect the speed of the ball at point 3? Explain.

(c) If the length of the string is changed (while keeping the angles the same), how will this affect the speed of the ball at point 3? Explain.

Reflection

R1. Compare your sketches of the net force for the three systems analyzed in part A.

R2. Why do some systems oscillate while others do not?

R3. What other oscillating systems can you identify?

R4. (a) Is a swinging pendulum (e.g., situations A3 and B3) ever in *dynamic equilibrium?* Explain.

(b) If the pendulum is never in dynamic equilibrium, why does it oscillate?

CS·25

Investigating the Period of Oscillatory Motion

Purpose and Expected Outcome

Some oscillatory motion is *periodic*, which means that each cycle or oscillation occurs in the same amount of time. This activity asks you to examine how various physical quantities such as the mass and spring constant affect the period of motion of an oscillating system. You will use Newton's laws as well as work and energy ideas to make predictions for a few simple systems. When possible you will test your predictions experimentally.

Prior Experience / Knowledge Needed

You should be familiar with the spring force, the gravitational force, the tension force, and Newton's laws of motion. Also, you will need definitions of *period* and *frequency*, which are provided below.

The **period** of oscillatory motion is the amount of time needed to complete one cycle. The symbol used for period is T, and its units are seconds.

The **frequency** of oscillatory motion is the number of cycles completed per second and is equal to the reciprocal of the period. The symbol used for frequency is f, and its units are Hertz (Hz), where 1Hz = 1 cycle per second = 1/s.

Explanation of Activity

Answer each of the following questions. Provide an explanation in each case. If possible, verify your answer experimentally.

PART A: Predicting Changes in the Period of Simple Systems

In each of the following situations a periodic or nearly periodic system is described. For each of the changes described, specify whether you think the period of the motion will increase, decrease, or remain the same, or that the answer cannot be determined.

A1. A cart is connected to a horizontal spring as shown. (Assume that the cart rolls without slipping.) The cart is moved to the right a distance d and released. The period is T. How does the period change when...

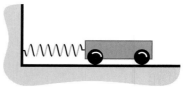

   (a) ... the mass of the cart is increased?

   (b) ... the spring is made stiffer, i.e., the spring constant is increased?

   (c) ... the spring is compressed a distance d and released from rest?

   (d) ... the spring is stretched farther than d?

   (e) ... the spring and cart system is taken to the Moon?

   (f) ... the spring's mass is increased?

A2. A block is connected to a vertical spring as shown. The block is pulled down a distance d and released from rest. How does the period change when...

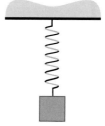

   (a) ... the mass of the block is increased?

   (b) ... the spring is made stiffer, i.e., the spring constant is increased?

   (c) ... the spring is compressed a distance d and released?

   (d) ... the spring and block system is taken to the Moon?

continued

A3. A ball is connected to the end of a suspended string to form a pendulum. The ball is displaced to the right through an angle θ and released from rest. How does the period change when...

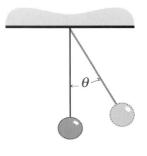

    (a) ... the mass of the ball is increased?

    (b) ... the string is made longer?

    (c) ... the ball is displaced to the right through an angle $\theta/2$ and released?

    (d) ... the pendulum is taken to the Moon?

A4. A super ball is bouncing off a level floor after being dropped from height d. Assume that very little energy is lost during each collision with the floor. How does the period change when...

    (a) ... the mass of the ball is increased?

    (b) ... the ball is dropped from a greater height?

    (c) Estimate the period for a super ball dropped from a height of 1 meter.

A5. A ball is connected to the end of a suspended string to form a pendulum. The ball is made to move in a circle with the string making an angle θ to the vertical. How does the period change when...

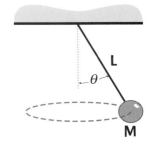

    (a) ... the mass of the ball is increased keeping L and θ the same (as the original system)?

    (b) ... the string is made longer keeping M and θ the same?

    (c) ... the angle is increased keeping L and M the same?

A6. A magnet is suspended by a thread and aligns itself with the magnetic field of the Earth. In the process of aligning itself, it oscillates several times about the final orientation. How does the period change when...

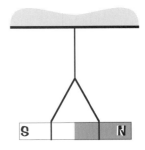
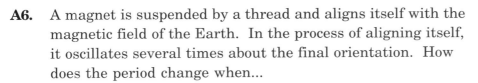

    (a) ... the mass of the magnet is increased?

    (b) ... the strength of the magnet is increased?

    (c) ... the length of the magnet is increased?

    (d) ... the strength of the Earth's magnetic field is increased?

PART B: Comparing Oscillating Systems

In each of the following you are presented with five systems. In each case order the systems according to the size of the period of oscillation, from smallest to largest.

B1. Identical carts are attached to identical springs in five different ways, as shown below.

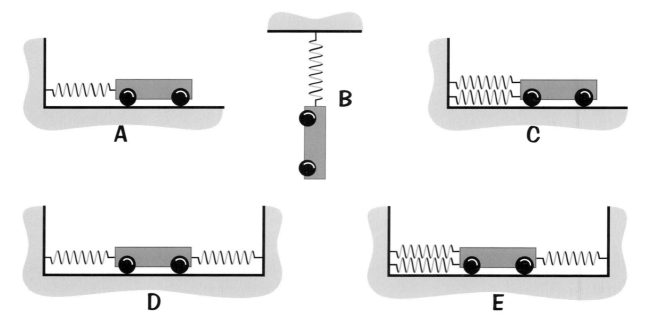

B2. Identical springs are attached to various objects, all having the <u>same mass</u>. Objects B and C are solid wheels, and object D is a bicycle wheel. For system E, the two carts are pushed together and released from rest at the same instant. Assume that all of the wheels roll without slipping and that no energy is dissipated due to friction.

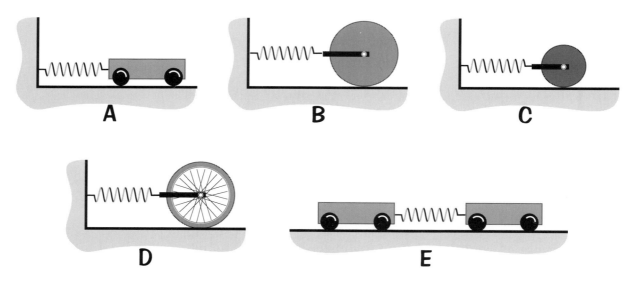

Reflection

R1. For which situations in Part A does the object oscillate about a point where the net force is zero?

R2. For which situations in Part A is the net force on the oscillating object <u>never</u> zero?

R3. For which situations in Part A does the net force on the oscillating object <u>always</u> point toward its equilibrium position?

R4. How is shortening the string of the pendulum in situation A3 like increasing the spring constant in situation A1? Examine each of the situations and determine whether there is any physical quantity that when varied is like varying the spring constant in situation A1.

R5. How is increasing the size of the disk in situation B2 like increasing the mass of the cart in situation A1? Examine each of the situations and determine whether there is any physical quantity that when varied is like varying the mass of the cart in situation A1.

Investigating Oscillations in Complex Systems

Purpose and Expected Outcome

Oscillations in complex systems and wave phenomena have many features in common. In this activity you will examine how a set of objects together can undergo oscillatory motion. This activity also serves as an intermediate stage toward understanding and describing *waves*, which is the topic of several upcoming activities.

Prior Experience / Knowledge Needed

You should understand the force laws for gravitation and springs, and you should know how to apply force and energy ideas. You should have some experience with oscillating systems, such as masses on springs and balls on strings.

Explanation of Activity

PART A: Oscillatory Motion for Systems with Two or Three Interacting Objects

In this part you will examine systems having several interacting objects and predict the circumstances, if any, under which the system will undergo oscillatory motion.

A1. (a) Two identical carts are connected by a spring. If the carts are pushed together and released at the same instant, will they undergo periodic motion?

(b) If your answer is Yes, indicate whether the period of motion would be larger, smaller, or the same as a single cart connected to a wall by the same spring. If your answer is No, explain why the motion cannot be periodic.

continued

A2. Two carts, A and B, are connected by three springs as shown below. The springs connected to the walls are identical to each other, but different from the spring that connects the two carts. If you displaced the carts in arbitrary ways and released them, generally they would undergo a very complicated motion.

Indicate at least two __different__ ways (meaning that the overall motion is different) you could displace the carts and release them so that the carts would undergo a *simple* oscillatory motion. (This means that both of the carts move with the same frequency.)

A3. Two pendulums, each made from a piece of string and a ball, are connected by a spring as shown. Indicate at least one way you could displace the balls so that they would undergo a simple oscillatory motion.

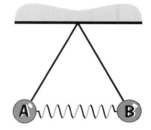

A4. Three identical carts, A, B and C, are connected by springs as shown. All the springs are identical to each other.

Indicate at least one way you could displace the carts and release them so that the carts would undergo a simple oscillatory motion.

PART B: Analyzing the Behavior of Systems with Many Interacting Objects

In this part you will examine a system having six identical balls (labeled 1 through 6) and 7 identical relaxed springs as shown below. Assume that all motion occurs on a horizontal frictionless surface. In each case one or more of the balls are displaced and you are asked to make sketches showing the positions of the balls at later times.

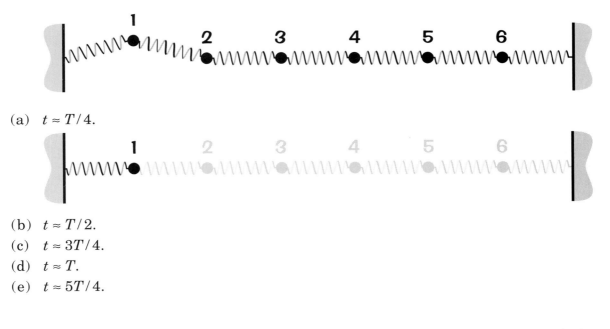

> Hint for making the sketches: At each instant, look at the force on each ball and the ball's velocity to predict where it will be at the next instant. You are not expected to be overly precise.

B1. Ball 1 is displaced upward a small amount and released from rest at $t = 0$ as shown below. The position of ball 1 is shown a short time later. (a) On a copy of the diagram, complete the sketch for $t \approx T/4$, then (b–e) draw sketches for the other times indicated.

(a) $t \approx T/4$.

(b) $t \approx T/2$.

(c) $t \approx 3T/4$.

(d) $t \approx T$.

(e) $t \approx 5T/4$.

continued

B2. All six balls are displaced upward by different amounts as shown and released. Assume that the system returns to this arrangement at $t = T$. Sketch the positions of the balls at the instants listed below.

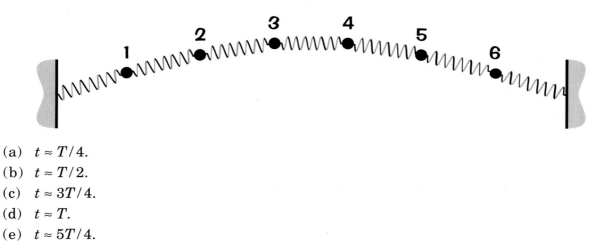

(a) $t \approx T/4$.
(b) $t \approx T/2$.
(c) $t \approx 3T/4$.
(d) $t \approx T$.
(e) $t \approx 5T/4$.

B3. Ball 1 is displaced to the left, while ball 2 is held fixed, as shown below. Both are released from rest at $t = 0$. Assume that ball 1 returns to its equilibrium position a short time later at $t = t_0$. Sketch the positions of the balls at the instants listed below.

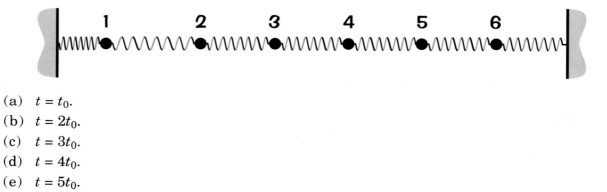

(a) $t = t_0$.
(b) $t = 2t_0$.
(c) $t = 3t_0$.
(d) $t = 4t_0$.
(e) $t = 5t_0$.

B4. Balls 3 and 4 are pushed together as far as possible and released from rest at $t = 0$. Assume that ball 3 returns to its equilibrium position a short time later at $t = t_0$. Sketch the positions of the balls at the four equally spaced instants listed below.

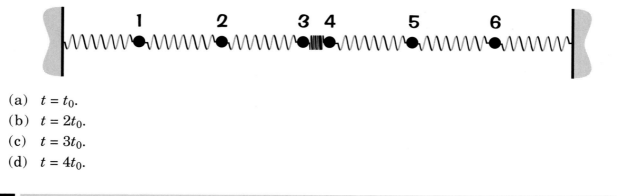

(a) $t = t_0$.
(b) $t = 2t_0$.
(c) $t = 3t_0$.
(d) $t = 4t_0$.

Reflection

R1. Why is it difficult to get simple oscillatory motion when there are many objects interacting?

R2. In situation B1, what kind of energy is present initially and where is the energy located? What happens to the energy as time passes?

R3. In situation B2, what kind of energy is present initially and where is the energy located? What happens to the energy as time passes?

R4. Do any of your sketches for Part B suggest simple oscillatory motion? If so, do you think the period of oscillation is larger than, smaller than, or the same as a single ball connected to one spring? If not, can you think of any way you might be able to get simple oscillatory motion?

Investigating Continuous Complex Systems

Purpose and Expected Outcome

In the previous activity you examined oscillatory motion in complex systems that contain only a few objects, usually connected by springs. Here you will explore oscillatory motion in materials such as strings, springs, and solid metals. These materials have an extremely large number of particles closely packed together. For many purposes, these materials can be thought of as continuous systems. In this activity you will learn how mass density, tension, and size affect the frequency of oscillation in continuous systems.

Prior Experience / Knowledge Needed

You should be familiar with the content of the prior activities on oscillatory motion.

SUMMARY OF RESULTS FOR OSCILLATORY MOTION

The **frequency** (or its reciprocal, the **period)** of oscillation for an object attached to a spring is determined by two factors: (a) the elastic constant k of the spring, and (b) the mass m of the object. The stiffer the spring, the larger the force exerted on the object at each position. A larger force leads to a larger acceleration and velocity at each position, which in turn results in a higher frequency (shorter period) of oscillation. The mass of an object determines its response to the force exerted by the spring. The larger the mass, the smaller the acceleration and velocity at each point, which in turn results in a lower frequency (longer period) of oscillation.

CONTINUOUS COMPLEX SYSTEMS

A *continuous* complex system (CCS) is one in which the components are so close together that we cannot perceive them as separate objects. For instance, a vibrating guitar string is an example of a continuous complex system because we cannot perceive that the individual parts of the string are moving differently.

We can model CCSs by imagining or constructing *discrete* systems containing objects and springs. The objects represent the components that make up the continuous system, and the springs represent the interactions between the components. Consider the system below in which the two carts have the same mass and the springs attached to the walls are identical.

Simple oscillatory motion will occur only when the carts are displaced the <u>same</u> amount from equilibrium and then released. If they are displaced in the same direction (left or right) the frequency observed is different (lower) than when the carts are displaced in opposite directions. This difference is due to the fact that the middle spring is involved in the second motion but not in the first.

RELATIONSHIP BETWEEN OSCILLATIONS AND SOUND

When you strum a guitar string, blow into a flute, or hit a tuning fork with a rubber mallet, you hear a sound. The reason is that these systems all undergo oscillations, thereby disturbing the air around them. The disturbance moves out through the air, eventually reaching your ear where it is sensed.

For some systems, such as a plucked guitar string, you can see the oscillations if you look carefully. By studying a large number of such systems, you would find that the quality of sound referred to as *pitch* is related to the frequency of oscillation. The relationship is somewhat complicated, but roughly speaking the higher the pitch of the sound, the larger the frequency (or equivalently the shorter the period) of oscillation in the system.

Most vibrating objects produce more than one sound frequency. In fact it is quite rare that an object will produce only one frequency. However, for many situations the pitch is determined by the lowest frequency of oscillation for the system, referred to as the *fundamental frequency*.

Materials Needed

- A set of tuning forks of the same material, but different sizes;
- some tuning forks made of different materials than the others;
- guitar strings, hanging masses, and pulleys;
- very large springs with relatively small spring constants; and
- recorders (a type of musical instrument) of different sizes.

Explanation of Activity

For each situation, you are asked to compare the frequency of oscillation for different conditions. For most situations you cannot directly observe the oscillations. If this is the case use your sense of pitch as a measure of frequency.

PART A: Investigating a Guitar String Under Tension

Attach one end of a guitar string to a secure wall or surface. Take the other end and pass it over a pulley. Hang one of the masses from the string. When the string is plucked, it vibrates with its *fundamental frequency* of oscillation, which we perceive as a certain pitch of sound.

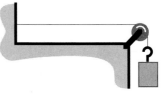

A1. What factors do you think might affect the string's frequency of oscillation (pitch)?

A2. Change the tension in the string. How does this affect the pitch you hear when you pluck the string?

A3. Change the angle that the string makes with the horizontal. How does this affect the pitch that you hear?

A4. Change the string's *mass density* (mass per unit length). How does this affect the pitch?

A5. Change the length of the vibrating part of the string. How does this affect the pitch? (**Suggestion:** If you place a wedge underneath the guitar string, and then press the string against the wedge with your finger, you can effectively change the length of the part of the string that oscillates without significantly changing the tension in the string.

A6. Investigate one of the other factors that you or your classmates mentioned above in A1.

PART B: Investigating Other Oscillating Systems

B1. For tuning forks of different sizes, but made of similar material, determine how the size of the tuning fork affects the frequency of oscillation. If possible, also compare tuning forks of the same size but made of different materials. Can you attribute any differences in the frequency of oscillation to mass density? What else might account for the difference in the frequency of oscillation of two tuning forks made of different materials?

B2. For different recorders (flute-like instruments with a whistle-like mouthpiece) investigate how size and finger placement affect the frequency of oscillation. Does the frequency depend on how hard you blow? What other factors affect the frequency?

B3. When a rubber band is stretched it is under tension. Devise a method to investigate...

(a) ... how the ratio of the tension to mass density affects the frequency of oscillation of the rubber band.

(b) ... how the length of the rubber band affects its frequency of oscillation.

Reflection

R1. (a) In part A, what factors determine the tension in the guitar string? Explain.

(b) In part A, what factors determine its frequency of oscillation? Explain.

R2. Describe in words any relationships you found between the frequency of oscillation and (a) mass density, (b) tension, and (c) size of the system. Do you think these relationships will hold for all continuous oscillating systems?

R3. Do any of the observed relationships seem reasonable to you? Can you explain any of the relationships? Do so, if you can.

R4. What principles can you use to determine how the mass and elastic constant affect the frequency of oscillation for an object hanging from a spring? Can you apply these same principles to a continuous system? Explain.

R5. Is there any quantity for a recorder that is like mass density for a string? If so, what is it?

CS·28

Recognizing the Role of Forces in Transverse Waves

Purpose and Expected Outcome

In this activity you will investigate transverse waves on strings and springs under tension. As in the previous activities you will analyze the forces producing the behavior. After completing this activity you will have a better understanding of the aspects of wave behavior that are similar to oscillatory behavior.

Prior Experience / Knowledge Needed

You should be familiar with discrete oscillating systems, such as objects connected to springs. You should also have some experience with continuous oscillating systems, such as vibrating guitar strings.

TRANSVERSE WAVES

A *transverse* wave is one that travels through a *medium* in a direction that is perpendicular to the motion of the individual components of the medium. For instance, consider a string under tension, as shown above to the right. If the string is disturbed upward near the right end, a wave will travel to the left, as shown in the sequence to the right. (For an *ideal* string, the wave will retain its shape and move with constant speed.) In this case, the medium is the string, and the wave is transverse because the motion of the wave (to the left) is perpendicular to the motion of the components of the medium (up and down).

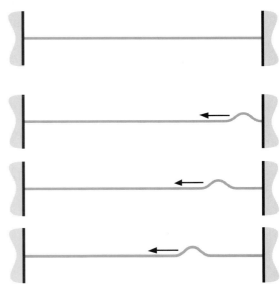

© 2001 Kendall/Hunt Publishing Company

Explanation of Activity

You will analyze the forces and motion of a segment of a string under different conditions. Assume that the string has a uniform mass density and constant tension throughout its length.

PART A. Relating Forces to the Motion of the String

A1. Consider the short segment of the string shown inside the dashed box below. Assume that the string is in equilibrium and that the boxed segment has mass m and length L.

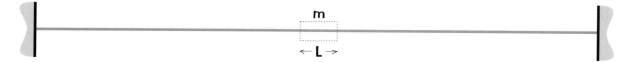

(a) Draw a free-body diagram for the piece of string.

(b) Is your free-body diagram consistent with no net force on the piece of string inside the box? Explain.

(c) Do your answers depend upon the location of the segment along the string?

A2. The string is displaced into the shape shown below and released. Consider the boxed segment of the string. Assume that the segment has mass m and length L.

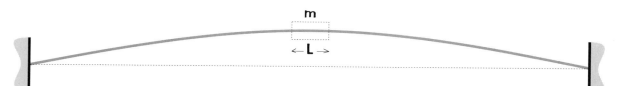

(a) Draw a free-body diagram for the boxed segment of string.

(b) Does your free-body diagram indicate that there is a net force on this segment? If so, what is the direction of the net force?

(c) How would the net force be different if the string had been pulled down (rather than up) the same distance?

continued

A3. The string is displaced into the same shape shown previously in A2 and released. The diagram below shows the string at subsequent instants of time after release. Consider the short segment of string of mass m that moves inside the dashed box. Be prepared to explain your answers. (**Note:** 1ms = 1 millisecond = 0.001s = 10^{-3} s.)

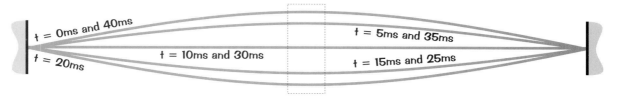

(a) At which time(s) is the net force greatest on the boxed segment?

(b) At which time(s) is the acceleration of the segment the greatest?

(c) At which time(s) is the speed of the segment the greatest?

(d) Does the shape of the string determine the net force on the segment? Does the shape of the string determine the acceleration of the segment?

(e) Does the shape of the string determine the direction of motion of the segment? Does the shape of the string determine the speed of the segment?

(f) If the tension in the string were increased, how would the rate at which the string moves up and down change? Would it increase, decrease, stay the same, or be undetermined?

(g) If the mass of the string were increased, but the length of string remained the same, how would the rate at which the string moves up and down change? Would it increase, decrease, stay the same, or be undetermined?

A4. Two people hold onto opposite ends of a stretched <u>spring</u>. One end of the spring is given a shake and a wave form travels down the spring as shown. Be prepared to explain your answers. (**Note:** 1ms = 1 millisecond = 0.001s = 10^{-3} s.)

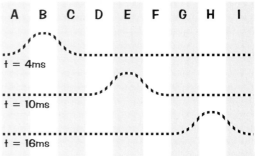

(a) At t = 10ms, what is the direction of the net force on each labeled piece of spring?

(b) At t = 10ms, what direction does each labeled piece of spring move? Is the net force on each labeled piece of spring always in the direction of motion?

(c) What direction does the wave move? Is there a net force on the wave? If so, in what direction?

(d) If the spring were stretched more before creating the wave, how would the speed of the wave change? Would it increase, decrease, stay the same, or be undetermined?

(e) If the spring were more massive, but its spring constant and length remained the same, how would the speed of the wave change? Would it increase, decrease, stay the same, or be undetermined?

PART B. Relating Forces to Variations in the Properties of the String

B1. Consider two strings each under tension between two walls. Both strings are displaced upward the same amount from equilibrium and then released. The only difference between the two situations is that the string on the bottom has twice the mass of the other.

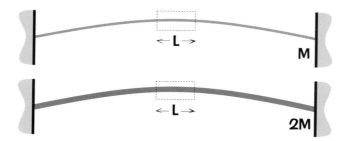

(a) Consider the forces on the boxed portion of string in each case. For which piece of string is the net force larger? How do the directions of the net forces compare?

(b) Consider the accelerations of the boxed portions of string? For which piece is the acceleration larger? How do the directions of the accelerations compare?

(c) Based on your understanding of dynamics and kinematics, which string would have the higher frequency of oscillation?

B2. Consider two strings each under tension between two walls. Both strings are displaced upward the same amount from equilibrium and then released. The only difference between the two situations is that the tension in the string on the bottom is twice as large as the tension in the other.

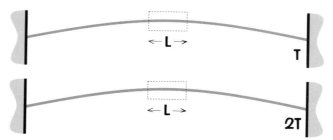

(a) Consider the forces on the boxed portion of string in each case. For which piece is the net force larger? How do the directions of the net forces compare?

(b) Consider the accelerations of the boxed portions of string? For which piece is the acceleration larger? How do the directions of the accelerations compare?

(c) Based on your understanding of dynamics and kinematics, which string would have the higher frequency of oscillation?

continued

B3. Consider two strings each under tension between two walls. Both strings are displaced upward the same amount from equilibrium and then released. Both the tension and the mass for the bottom string are twice those of the other string.

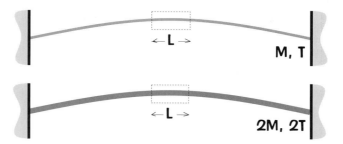

(a) Consider the forces on the boxed portion of string in each case. For which piece is the net force larger? How do the directions of the net forces compare?

(b) Consider the accelerations of the boxed portions of string? For which piece is the acceleration larger? How do the directions of the accelerations compare?

(c) Based on your understanding of dynamics and kinematics, which string would have the higher frequency of oscillation?

B4. Consider two strings each under tension between two walls. Both strings are displaced upward the same amount from equilibrium and then released. The only difference between the two situations is that the lower string is twice as long as the other. (This means that the total mass of the longer string is also twice as great, but the tensions are kept the same.)

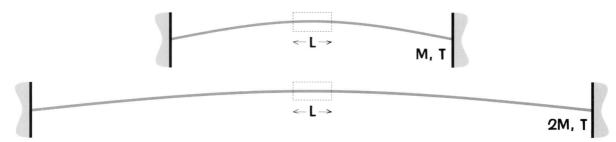

(a) Consider the masses of the boxed portion of string in each case. (At equilibrium both pieces of string are the same size.) For which piece is the mass larger?

(b) Consider the forces on the boxed portion of string in each case. For which piece is the net force larger? How do the directions of the net forces compare?

(c) Consider the accelerations of the boxed portions of string? For which piece is the acceleration larger? How do the directions of the accelerations compare?

(d) Based on your understanding of dynamics and kinematics, which string would have the highest frequency of oscillation?

Reflection

R1. Reconsider the spring from situation A4. If the wave form was made in the middle of the spring and released, what do you think would happen? If you think it moves to the right in the same way it did for situation A4 indicate how the wave "knows" to move to the right and not to the left. If you think it moves in a different way explain how and why it moves differently.

R2. For situation A4, how does the motion of the pieces of spring compare with the motion of the wave?

R3. In the previous activity you made observations to determine how various factors such as tension, mass density, and size affected the frequency of oscillation in continuous systems. Were your observations consistent with your analysis in this activity using forces?

R4. A drum head will vibrate when hit. What are some of the factors that will determine the frequency of vibration?

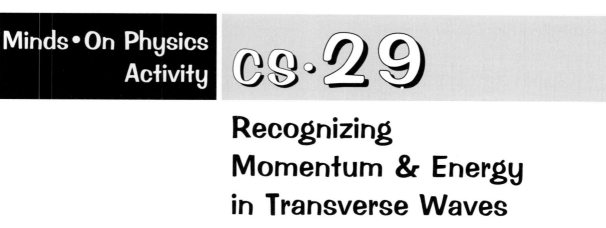

Recognizing Momentum & Energy in Transverse Waves

Purpose and Expected Outcome

In the previous activity you examined how forces in a material medium, such as a string or spring, give rise to wave motion. In this activity you will examine the role of momentum, energy, and energy transfer in wave motion. You will use momentum and energy principles to make predictions about the motion of waves.

Prior Experience / Knowledge Needed

You should understand momentum and the two basic forms of energy: kinetic and potential. You should know the Work–Kinetic Energy and Impulse–Momentum Theorems, as well as the principle of Conservation of Energy. Before starting this activity consider the energy in a system of objects connected by springs. Use the model of objects-connected-by-springs to help you to think about the energy contained in wave motion.

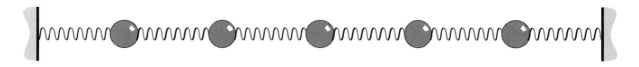

As you might have seen previously, any displacement of one of the masses from its equilibrium position would cause the adjacent springs to be stretched or compressed. These springs would apply forces on adjacent masses, causing them to move. In this way motion and energy is transmitted through the system of masses.

Explanation of Activity

In each of the following six situations there is wave motion. For each situation answer questions about the energy and momentum contained in the wave. Be prepared to explain how you determined your answer.

SITUATION A. A Vibrating String

A string is displaced into the shape shown below (t = 0ms) and released. The diagram below shows the string at subsequent instants of time after release. Five segments, labeled J–N, are indicated by the alternating white and gray rectangles. (**Note:** 1ms = 1 millisecond = 10^{-3}s = 0.001s)

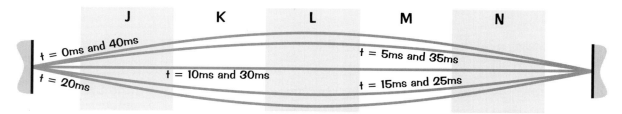

A1. For each of the labeled segments of the string...

    (a) ... when is its total potential energy the largest? the smallest? Explain.

    (b) ... when is its total kinetic energy the largest? the smallest? Explain.

    (c) ... when is its total momentum the largest? the smallest? What is the direction of the total momentum?

A2. At time t = 0ms, which segment(s) of the string has the largest potential energy? the largest kinetic energy? Explain.

A3. At time t = 10ms, which segment of the string has the largest potential energy? the largest kinetic energy? Explain.

A4. Is the total momentum of the string changing? Explain.

A5. Is the energy in each segment of string conserved? Explain.

SITUATION B. A Transverse Wave on a Spring

Two people hold onto opposite ends of a stretched <u>spring</u>. One end of the spring is given a shake and a form travels down the spring as shown. The spring is divided into 9 segments, labeled R–Z. (**Note:** 1ms = 1 millisecond = 10^{-3}s = 0.001s)

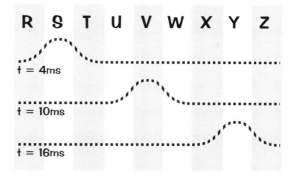

B1. For each of the 9 labeled segments of string...

    (a)   ... when is the total potential energy the largest? the smallest? Explain.

    (b)   ... when is the total kinetic energy the largest? the smallest? Explain.

    (c)   ... when is the total momentum the largest? the smallest? What is the direction of the total momentum at t = 10ms?

B2. At t = 10ms, which segment of the spring has the largest potential energy? the largest kinetic energy? Explain.

B3. When is the kinetic energy of segment V the largest? When is the potential energy of segment V the largest? Explain.

B4. Is the total momentum of the spring changing? Explain.

B5. Is the energy in each segment of spring conserved? Explain.

SITUATION C. Two Vibrating Strings with Different Masses

Consider two strings, A and B, each under tension between two walls. Both strings are displaced upward the same amount from equilibrium and released. The only difference between the two strings is that the one on the bottom has twice the mass of the other.

C1. Which string has the larger total energy?

C2. Which string has the larger maximum potential energy? the larger maximum kinetic energy?

C3. Which string has the larger total momentum at each moment?

C4. Based on your understanding of energy, which string would have the larger period of oscillation?

SITUATION D. Two Vibrating Strings with Different Tensions

Consider two strings, A and B, each under tension between two walls. Both strings are displaced upward the same amount from equilibrium and released. The only difference between the two strings is that the tension in the one on the bottom is twice as large as the tension in the other.

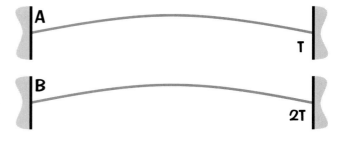

D1. Which string has the larger total energy?

D2. Which string has the larger maximum potential energy? the larger maximum kinetic energy?

D3. Which string has the larger total momentum when it is horizontal?

D4. Based on your understanding of energy, which string would have the larger period of oscillation?

SITUATION E. Two Vibrating Strings with Different Masses and Tensions

Consider two strings, A and B, each under tension between two walls. Both strings are displaced upward the same amount from equilibrium and released. Both the tension and the mass for the bottom string are twice those of the other string.

E1. Which string has the larger total energy? the larger maximum potential energy? the larger maximum kinetic energy?

E2. Which string has the larger total momentum at each moment?

E3. Based on your understanding of energy, which string would have the larger period of oscillation?

SITUATION F. Two Vibrating Strings with Different Lengths

Consider two strings each under tension between two walls. Both strings are displaced upward the same amount from equilibrium and then released. The only difference between the two situations is that string B is twice as long as string A. (This means that the total mass of string B is also twice as large as string A, but the tensions are kept the same.)

F1. Which string has the larger total energy per length of string?

F2. Which string has the larger maximum potential energy per length of string? the larger maximum kinetic energy per length of string?

F3. When the momentum of each string is maximum, which has the larger total momentum per length of string?

F4. Based on your understanding of energy, which string would have the larger period of oscillation?

Reflection

R1. How does the mass density of a wave medium (rope, spring, etc.) influence the period and/or velocity of waves in the medium? Do you think the same relationship would hold for other wave media? Give some examples.

R2. How does the tension in a wave medium influence the period and/or velocity of waves in the medium? Do you think the same relationship would hold for other wave media? Give some examples.

R3. Do you reach the same conclusions about the frequency of oscillation with energy concepts as with force concepts? Which concepts did you find easier to use?

R4. Use dimensional analysis to determine how the speed of a wave depends upon the tension and mass density of a spring, such as the one used in situation B. Is the result consistent with your analysis and observations so far? Use your result to estimate the speed of a wave for a particular spring, and then test to see how good your estimate is.

Analyzing Simple Wave Behavior

Purpose and Expected Outcome

There are many different types of waves with a diverse set of behaviors. However, some wave behaviors are fairly common. In this activity you will learn about three such wave behaviors: Reflection, Transmission, and Interference. You will learn about these behaviors by analyzing waves in a few simple situations using basic principles from mechanics.

Prior Experience / Knowledge Needed

You should be familiar with all of the prior activities on waves, particularly the last two, which dealt with forces, momentum, and energy in transverse waves. You should be prepared to apply the major principles of dynamics.

Explanation of Activity

Each of the following situations deal with one or more wave behaviors. You will be asked a set of questions about force, momentum, and energy. Based on your analysis you will be asked to make a prediction about the wave behavior. When possible check your predictions by making direct observations of the behavior.

SITUATION A: A Simple Mechanical System

The following mechanical system provides some useful analogies for looking at the way waves reflect and transmit energy at a boundary.

Consider a series of carts with attached springs, some of which are shown below. The carts undergo sequential collisions, starting with the two carts on the far left. Assume that each collision is completely over before the next one begins. You are asked to give descriptions of what will happen to the system under various conditions. Be sure to give some indication of the relative sizes of velocities and the relative positions of any moving carts. The moving cart has speed v just before it hits the next one.

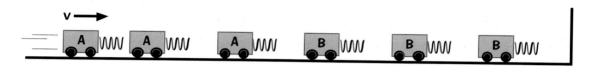

A1. Describe what will happen if the masses of all the carts are the same.

A2. Describe what will happen if the masses of the carts labeled A are smaller than the masses of carts labeled B.

A3. Describe what will happen if the masses of the carts labeled A are larger than the masses of carts labeled B.

A4. Under what conditions is energy conserved? Explain.

A5. Is momentum conserved? Explain.

SITUATION B: Reflection of a Wave at a Boundary

This part investigates what happens when a wave "collides" with a wall to which it is attached.

One end of a spring is attached to a wall. With the spring stretched the opposite end is given a shake, sending a wave down the spring toward the wall.

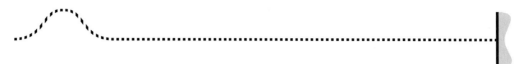

B1. Does the wall do work on the spring at any time? (If so, is it positive or negative?) Does the wall do net work on the spring? (If so, is it positive or negative?)

B2. Does the wall deliver an impulse to the spring at any time? (If so, in what direction?) Can the wall provide a net impulse? (If so, in what direction?)

B3. Sketch a graph of the force that the wall exerts on the spring as a function of time. Is your graph consistent with B2?

B4. Underneath the graph from B3, sketch the height of the wave as a function of time for a point just to the left of the wall. Are your two graphs consistent? Explain.

B5. What do you think will happen after the wave collides with the wall? How is it similar to, and different from, the original wave form?

SITUATION C: Reflection and Transmission of a Wave Entering a More Dense Medium

Two springs are connected together. One end is connected to a wall. With the springs stretched, the free end is given a shake. Assume that spring 2 has a larger mass density than spring 1. The tension is the same in both springs.

C1. **Work:** Is net work done on the heavier spring by the lighter one? (If so, is it positive or negative?) Compare with the net work done on the lighter spring by the heavier one.

C2. **Impulse:** Does the lighter spring deliver a net impulse to the heavier one? (If so, in what direction?) Compare with the net impulse delivered to the lighter spring by the heavier one.

C3. **Kinetic Energy:** Will the wave form on the heavier spring move faster or slower than the original wave form on the lighter spring? Explain.

C4. **Potential Energy:** Will the wave form on the heavier spring have a larger or smaller height (amplitude) than the original wave form? Explain.

C5. **Limiting Cases:** What would happen if the two springs had the same mass density? What would happen if the second spring had a very large mass density?

C6. **Prediction:** Sketch the wave after it has reached the second spring, but before it has reached the wall. Compare with the original wave form.

SITUATION D: Reflection and Transmission of a Wave Entering a Less Dense Medium

This part investigates what happens when a wave on a spring "collides" with a second less massive spring, which is attached to the first.

Two springs are connected together. One end is connected to a wall. With the springs stretched, the free end is given a shake. Assume spring 2 is less massive than spring 1. The tension is the same in both springs.

D1. **Work:** Is net work done on the lighter spring by the heavier one? (If so, is it positive or negative?) Compare with the net work done on the heavier spring by the lighter one.

D2. **Impulse:** Does the heavier spring deliver a net impulse to the lighter one? (If so, in what direction?) Compare with the net impulse delivered to the heavier spring by the lighter one.

D3. **Kinetic Energy:** Will the wave form on the heavier spring move faster or slower than the original wave form on the lighter spring? Explain.

D4. **Potential Energy:** Will the wave form on the heavier spring have a greater height (amplitude) than the original wave form? Explain.

D5. **Limiting Cases:** What would happen if the two springs had the same mass density? What would happen if the second spring had a very, very small mass density?

D6. **Prediction:** Sketch the wave after it has reached the second spring, but before it has reached the wall. Compare with the original wave form.

SITUATION E: Interference Between Identical Wave Forms

Consider the case of two upright wave forms moving toward each other as shown below.

A spring is stretched, and identical wave disturbances are set up at each end, as shown. The two wave forms travel toward each other. When they completely overlap, the waves add so that the peak is twice as high. Later the two wave forms emerge seemingly unchanged by their interaction with one another.

E1. When is the total potential energy the largest? (**Hint:** Consider the model of many masses connect by springs.)

E2. When is the total kinetic energy the largest?

E3. Can the kinetic energy ever be zero? Explain. Can the potential energy ever be zero? Explain.

E4. When is the total momentum the largest? ... the smallest? What is the direction of the total momentum?

$t = t_1$

$t = t_2$

$t = t_3$

$t = t_4$

$t = t_5$

E5. Is the total energy conserved? Explain.

E6. Is the total momentum conserved? Explain.

E7. If you made the combined wave form by displacing the spring into the shape shown at $t = t_3$ and then releasing it from rest, what would happen? Is your answer consistent with your previous answers?

SITUATION F: Interference Between Two Wave Forms with One Inverted

We now consider the case in which one of the wave forms is inverted relative to the other as shown below.

A spring is stretched, and identical wave forms, one upright, the other upside-down, are set up at each end as shown. The two wave forms travel toward each other. When they completely overlap, the spring is essentially straight. Later the two wave forms emerge, seemingly unchanged by their interaction with one another.

F1. When is the total potential energy the largest? ... the smallest? Explain.

F2. When is the total kinetic energy the largest?

F3. Can the kinetic energy ever be zero? Explain. Can the potential energy ever be zero? Explain.

F4. When is the total momentum the largest? the smallest? What is the direction of the total momentum?

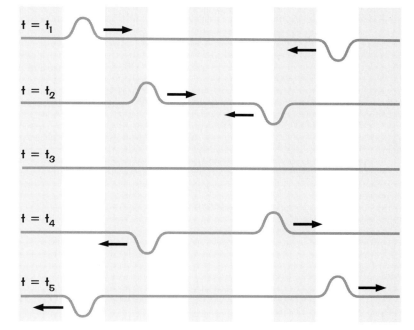

F5. Is the total energy conserved? Explain.

F6. Is the total momentum conserved? Explain.

F7. The combined wave form is a flat string at $t = t_3$. How do the two wave forms emerge from a flat string? Is your answer consistent with your previous answers?

Reflection

R1. Can a wave form ever have zero momentum? Can a wave form ever have zero total energy? Can a wave form ever have zero potential energy? What about zero kinetic energy?

R2. Two carts roll toward each other frictionlessly and collide. How does the behavior of the carts compare with the behavior of the wave forms in situation E. How would your answers to the questions in Situation E change if they referred to the carts rather than the wave forms?

R3. When a wave hits a boundary, as in situation B, the reflected wave is inverted relative to the incoming wave. (See below.)

To create an inverted wave moving in the opposite direction, is it necessary to do work? If so, what force does the work? Is it necessary to deliver an impulse? If so, what force delivers the impulse? Explain.

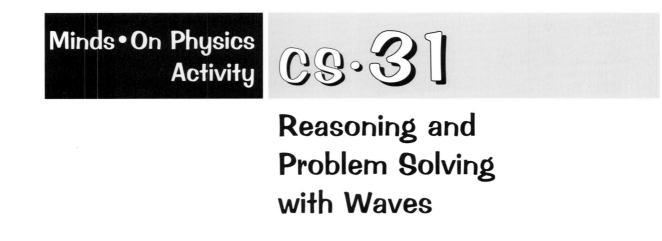

Minds•On Physics Activity
cs·31

Reasoning and Problem Solving with Waves

Purpose and Expected Outcome

In this activity you will use Newton's Laws, Work–Kinetic Energy, Impulse–Momentum and Conservation of Energy to reason about situations and solve problems involving waves.

Prior Experience / Knowledge Needed

You should be familiar with the wave phenomena and with the basic principles of mechanics.

Explanation of Activity

For each situation answer the questions asked and provide an explanation of your answers in terms of force, energy, and/or momentum concepts. Consider drawing free-body diagrams for each situation you investigate. Determine whether any forces are doing work or delivering an impulse. When comparing waves under different conditions determine whether there are any differences in the amounts of potential and kinetic energy at various times. In the first part, you will work with relatively simple systems. Then in the second part, you will attempt to predict and/or explain what will happen in more complicated situations.

PART A: Analyzing 'Simple' Complex Systems

A1. On a stringed instrument such as a guitar, the tension in the string is adjusted until it produces a particular sound when strummed. Once the desired tension is achieved, other notes are produced by pressing the string at various positions along the neck of the guitar.

   (a) Why does pressing on the string at different points change the sound produced by the guitar?

   (b) For a tuned string, how would you increase the pitch? How would you decrease the pitch? Is there any limit on how high or how low a pitch you can achieve?

   (c) On a six string guitar, the strings are different thicknesses. Which strings are fatter? Why? What is the impact of thickness on the sound produced by the strings?

A2. Rank the following situations from lowest to highest according to the period of oscillation of the string. Assume that all strings have the same length and mass density. Explain your reasoning.

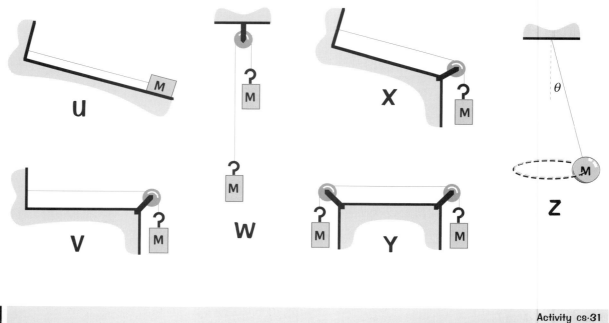

A3. A mechanical vibrator is connected to a string as shown. The mechanical vibrator can be used to cause the string to vibrate at different frequencies.

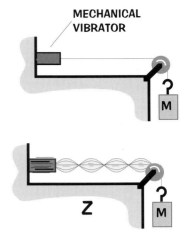

It is found that only certain frequencies of the vibrator will produce simple periodic wave motion on the string. Three of the wave forms that can be produced are shown below.

(a) While the string is vibrating, is there ever an instant when the entire string is at rest? If so, for each situation above, draw the string at that instant.

(b) While the string is vibrating, is the speed of the string changing? If so, for each situation, draw the string at the instant when the speed of the string is maximum.

(c) While the string is vibrating, is the speed of the string the same everywhere along the string? If not, indicate where the speed of the string is smallest and largest, and indicate where the speed of the string is <u>always</u> zero.

(d) Order these wave forms from shortest period to longest period (or equivalently, from highest to lowest frequency). Explain your reasoning.

(e) If the hanging mass is made heavier, how would the period of each wave form change?

(f) If the string is made longer, how would the period for each wave form change?

(g) Predict the shapes of other possible wave forms based on any patterns you perceive. Sketch three of them. Why do these wave forms exist and others do not?

continued

A4. In a previous activity you were asked in a reflection question to do a dimensional analysis to come up with the speed of a wave in terms of the tension and mass density of a string or spring. You should have found that the combination:

$$\sqrt{\frac{F_T}{M/L}}$$

has the dimensions of speed, where F_T is the tension and M/L is the mass density.

(a) For a particular spring, estimate the speed of a wave at a given tension and mass density. Describe how you made the estimate.

(b) Check your estimate.

(c) Try a few more cases. Are you able to conclude anything about your method of estimating the speed of the wave?

A5. Consider a block hanging from a spring. The block is displaced upward and released. The frequency of oscillation for the system is 2 cycles/second. Starting at $t = \frac{1}{2}$ s, a small force (much smaller than the maximum spring force) is applied to the block in the vertical direction. The force is applied in four different ways:

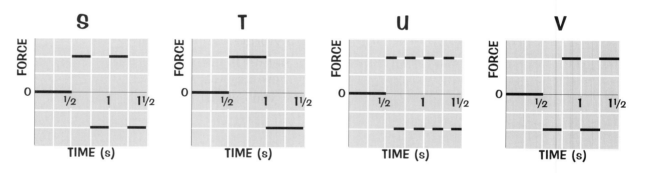

(a) In which case(s) will the largest amount of energy be transferred to the block and spring? (**Hint:** Look at the work done by the applied force.)

(b) In which case(s) will the smallest amount of energy be transferred to the block and spring? Explain.

(c) Formulate a principle which describes how to maximize the transfer of energy to a system using a variable force as was done here.

A6. Two pieces of 32-gauge wire are found in a drawer and each is used to make the set-up shown to the right. The two wires have the same thickness, about 0.2mm. It is determined that no matter what mass M is hung from the wires, the ratio of the vibrational frequencies of the two wires is the same, about $9/5$.

(a) Why do you suppose the ratio of frequencies does not depend on M?

(b) What can you say about the two wires?

PART B: Analyzing 'Complicated' Complex Systems

B1. Describe how a playground swing works. Can you transfer energy to the swing while you are on it? If so, how do you transfer the maximum amount of energy to the swing per amount of effort? Analyze a videotape of someone swinging in different ways and see if your explanation is valid.

B2. Get a set of tuning forks and arrange them according to pitch. (If possible, use some made of the same material and some made of different material.) Take one tuning fork (preferably with a pitch in the middle so that there are about as many with a higher frequency as with a lower frequency) and place it alone on a firm horizontal surface. Predict what will happen if one of the other tuning forks is hit with a mallet and brought close to the isolated tuning fork. Will what happens depend upon which tuning fork is used? Explain, and then test your predictions.

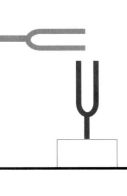

B3. An open glass tube is partially submerged in water. At the top end of a glass tube, a tuning fork is made to vibrate. Move the tube up and down slowly keeping the tuning fork just above the end of the tube. What do you observe? Is there any interaction? Is there any transfer of energy? How would you explain your observations?

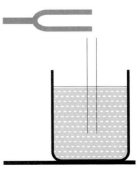

B4. Explain why when rows of soldiers in a long column cross a bridge, they are told to stop marching in unison. Does it seem possible that marching in unison could be dangerous? Explain. What can you say about the natural frequency of oscillation of any bridges susceptible to damage?

B5. Explain how it is possible to shatter a wine glass by singing a note. Do you think some glasses would be easier to break than others? Explain. Can you think of any ways to determine the frequency of sound needed to break a particular glass?

Reflection

R1. What factors affect the frequency of sound emitted by a string?

R2. Reconsider problem A3.

(a) Is it possible to have an odd number of wave forms on the string? Why or why not?

(b) Compare your answers to those of your classmates. Resolve any differences.

R3. What factors influence how effectively energy can be transferred from one system to another?

R4. Electric guitars and acoustic guitars generate sound using different principles. Explain the difference.

R5. Describe some situations in which energy is transferred from one system to another via wave motion.

Reader

COMPLEX
SYSTEMS

COMPLEX SYSTEMS
READER
CHAPTER 1 FLUIDS

A *fluid* is something that has the ability to flow, for example, water, air, oil, steam, shampoo, and milk. The behavior of fluids is therefore different in many ways from the behavior of rigid objects. So far, you have only seen how to apply Newton's laws and the conservation laws to systems of rigid, non-rotating objects. In a fluid, the basic unit would therefore seem to be the atoms and molecules that make up the fluid. But there are so many of them that we can never hope to describe the behavior of the system by specifying and watching the positions, velocities, interactions, and accelerations of every one of them.

However, whether it is a glass of water or a box filled with air, this collection of uncountably many components behaves in remarkably predictable ways, because we can still apply Newton's laws and the laws of conservation of momentum and energy, even though these principles might seem to be more hidden than they were before. By introducing new concepts such as *density* and *pressure*, we begin to see patterns in how the system as a whole behaves. By applying Newton's laws and the conservation laws, we can successfully describe and understand many features of fluids.

This chapter has three sections. In the first, you will learn about the concepts of *density* and *pressure*. In the second, you will apply these ideas to *static fluids*, which means that the fluid is at rest (not moving). In the third, you will apply them to *moving fluids*.

1.1 DENSITY AND PRESSURE

Why do some objects float when put into a fluid, yet other objects sink? How can we predict the level of water in different circumstances? What is the best way to describe the properties of static and moving fluids? The answers to these and many other questions can be expressed most easily and usefully in terms of two new quantities: *density* and *pressure*.

1.1.1 Density. *Density* is a measure of how much mass is contained in a standard volume of material. The definition of *average density* is:

$$\rho_{\text{ave}} \equiv \frac{M_{\text{total}}}{V_{\text{total}}} \qquad \textbf{definition of average density}$$

where M_{total} is the total mass, and V_{total} is the total volume of an object. For instance, a baseball has a diameter of about 7cm (0.07m) and a mass of about 145g (0.145kg), so its volume is about 180cm^3 and its average density is about 0.8gm/cm^3. The symbol ρ (*rho*, pronounced "row") is used to denote density.

The standard MKS unit of density is kg/m^3, but these units can be awkward for many everyday objects, because 1 cubic meter (1m^3) of material is relatively large. For instance, in MKS units, a baseball has a volume of about 0.00018m^3 (1.8×10^{-4}m^3) and an average density of about 800kg/m^3.

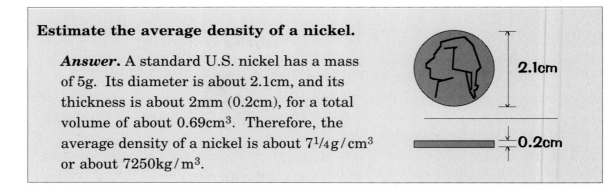

Estimate the average density of a nickel.

Answer. A standard U.S. nickel has a mass of 5g. Its diameter is about 2.1cm, and its thickness is about 2mm (0.2cm), for a total volume of about 0.69cm^3. Therefore, the average density of a nickel is about 7^1/$_4$g/cm^3 or about 7250kg/m^3.

2.1cm

0.2cm

In this example, we have used the volume of a disk, $V_{\text{disk}} = \pi r^2 h$, where r is the radius of the disk and h is its thickness.

To get a sense of how dense something is, we often compare its density to the density of water, which is 1g/cm^3 or 1000kg/m^3. The baseball is slightly less dense than water, because 0.8g/cm^3 is slightly smaller than 1g/cm^3. The nickel is much more dense than water, because 7g/cm^3 is much larger than 1g/cm^3.

Density is <u>not</u> a measure of how "thick" a fluid is. Imagine putting a spoon into a glass filled with water and trying to move the spoon. Now imagine putting a spoon into a glass filled with oil and trying to move the spoon. Better yet, go get two glasses, two spoons, some water and some oil and do it yourself. It is easier to move the spoon through the water, but water has a higher density than oil, which means that 1cm^3 of oil has a smaller mass than 1cm^3 of water. (The density of oil varies depending on its type, but it is usually about 0.8g/cm^3.)

1.1.2 Dependence of density on location or circumstances. The density of a substance does not generally depend on how much of it you have.

> ### What is the average density of <u>two</u> nickels?
>
> ***Answer.*** The same as one! Two nickels have twice the mass of one, but they also have twice the volume, so the average density remains the same, about $7^{1}/_{4}\,\text{g}/\text{cm}^3$.
>
> ### How much money would you have if you had a gallon of nickels?
>
> ***Answer.*** A gallon is 4 quarts, or about 4 liters, which is equal to $4000\,\text{cm}^3$. Ignoring the empty space between nickels, this is about 29,000g of nickels. At 5g per nickel, this is 5,800 nickels. At $0.05 per nickel, this is $290.

Note that sometimes you must be able to convert from one set of units to another, and there are many different units for volume. In the example above, we used 1gal = 4qt, 1qt = 0.95L ≈ 1L, and $1\text{L} = 1000\,\text{cm}^3$.

Gases have mass, so you must be careful when analyzing situations involving them.

> ### A basketball is inflated with the normal amount of air. Compare the average density of this basketball to a basketball inflated with twice the normal amount of air.
>
>
>
> ***Answer.*** The density of the basketball with twice as much air in it is slightly larger than the density of the basketball with the normal amount of air. Assuming the volumes of the two basketballs are the same, the basketball with more air in it has the larger mass, so it also has the larger density. The increase in mass is small, however, so its density is only slightly larger.

The amount of mass in a closed system is constant under most conditions. The volume of a certain amount of material generally changes under varying conditions, such as changing pressure and temperature. Therefore, the density of a substance depends on the conditions. However, for a wide range of temperatures and pressures, most solids and liquids have roughly constant densities, so we can treat them as being constant. (Notable exceptions are bridges and roads whose densities change only slightly, but with noticeable effects on their dimensions.) So, for instance, water has the same density on the Moon as it has on the Earth.

Gases are different. Their densities depend greatly on temperature and pressure. So, for example, the density of air is very different at a high altitude than it is at sea level, because a certain mass of air has different volumes at the two locations.

Any substance whose density does not depend on pressure are called *incompressible*, because the volume of a certain amount of it does not change. Pure water is generally treated as incompressible, so that even at great depths, we can assume that its density is 1g/cm^3.

1.1.3 Distinguishing mass, weight, and density. It is easy to confuse the concepts of *mass*, *weight*, and *density*, because they are so closely related. But it is important—and often crucial—to keep them separate in your mind and in your conversations with others so that you can communicate clearly, apply principles properly, and solve problems successfully.

Mass is a quantity that determines how an object will respond to a force—for the same force, the larger the mass, the smaller the acceleration. It is measured in kilograms (kg) or grams (g) and its value does not generally depend on where the object is located. It is the same on the Earth, on the Moon, and in a space station. *Weight* is the total gravitational force exerted on an object; its value very much depends on where the object is located. *Density* is the amount of mass per standard unit of volume, such as grams per cubic centimeter (g/cm^3), kilograms per cubic meter (kg/m^3), or even kilograms per liter (kg/L). We can usually assume that the density of a pure liquid or solid does not depend on conditions—temperature, pressure, etc.—or on amount. However, density usually depends on the *state*—solid, liquid, gas, or plasma—of the substance.

So, for example, (a) 20g of steam has a larger mass and weight, but a smaller density, than 10g of water. (b) At the surface of the Earth, 100g of water and 100g of wood have the same mass and weight, but water has the larger density. (c) A piece of wood has the same mass, weight, and density whether or not it is floating in water. (d) A 100g block of wood at the surface of the Earth has a larger weight, but the same mass and density, as an identical block of wood at the surface of the Moon. (e) When you add helium to an empty fire extinguisher, it does not become lighter. It becomes heavier. The mass, weight, and density of the fire extinguisher all increase. And finally, (f) a balloon filled with helium has a larger mass and weight than an empty balloon, but a smaller density.

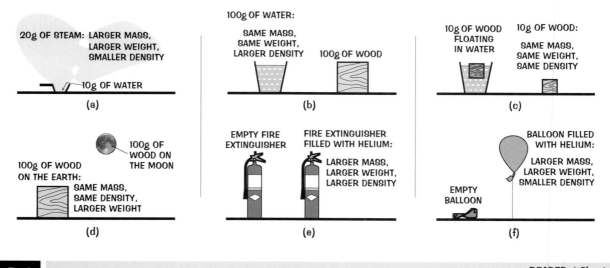

1.1.4 Pressure. Imagine a glass filled with water. There are billions of billions of millions of molecules of H_2O in the glass (that is, more than 10^{24} of them), pressing on each other and the inside of the glass and also bouncing off each other and the inside of the glass. The combined effect of all these water molecules pressing on the glass is a force perpendicular to its surface. In other words, there is a normal force exerted by the water on the inside of the glass. Even though this force is really a normal force, we usually refer to it instead as the *force due to water molecules under pressure* or simply the *force exerted by the water*.

Pressure is a measure of the normal force per unit of surface area. The definition of pressure is:

$$P \equiv \frac{F_N}{A} \quad (A \text{ planar})$$
                                                                    definition of pressure

where F_N is the normal force exerted by the fluid, and A is the *planar* area over which the force is exerted. (*Planar* means that the area is flat.) The symbol P is used to denote pressure. The standard MKS unit of pressure is the Pascal (Pa), which is equal to $1N/m^2$.

To find the force exerted by a fluid, multiply the pressure in the fluid by the area of the surface to find its strength. The direction is toward the surface, perpendicular to it. For instance, the pressure in the atmosphere at the surface of the Earth is about $100,000Pa$ or about $10N/cm^2$. (It is also about $15lb/in^2$ or about 15psi.)

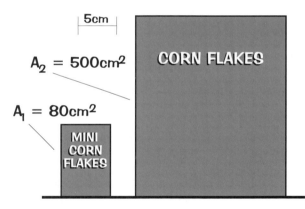

Let's compare two situations. You have two boxes of cereal, a single-serving size having dimensions 8cm × 10cm (or about 3in × 4in) and a family size having dimensions 20cm × 25cm (about 8in × 10in). The force exerted by air on the front of the small box is $10N/cm^2 \times 80cm^2 = 800N$ ($15lb/in^2 \times 12in^2 =$ 180lb), pointing straight into the page. The force exerted by air on the front of the large box is $10N/cm^2 \times 500cm^2 = 5,000N$ ($15lb/in^2$ × $80in^2 = 1,200lb$), also into the page. This is more than 6 times as large as the force on the small box. So, the pressure on both boxes is the same ($10N/cm^2$), but the force exerted on the larger box is much larger (5,000N vs. 800N).

Pressure is not a force. Fluid molecules <u>under pressure</u> exert forces on the molecules they touch, such as other fluid molecules or the surface of a container, table, wall, or box.

Why do the cereal boxes remain at rest when such large forces are exerted on them? Because the total force due to air pressure on all sides is zero (or very close to zero). If large forces are exerted on each surface, why does air pressure not crush the boxes? Because the forces of air pressure are exerted on both the outsides and the <u>insides</u> of each box. The forces on the insides of the box are pushing out, which prevents the box from being crushed by air pressure. However, if the air were removed from inside the boxes, then they would become crushed.

In the following example, we show how the force depends on the orientation of the surface.

A steel block has dimensions 2cm × 4cm × 5cm and a mass of about 340g. Air pressure is about 10N/cm². What is the force exerted by the air on each face of the block?

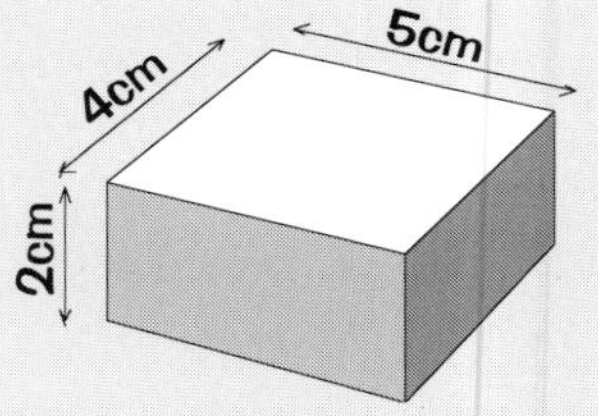

Answer. The force on each face depends on its area and orientation. So, for example, the force on the top is [200N, down] and the force on the bottom is [200N, up]. The forces on the other four faces are also proportional to their areas. The directions are easiest to describe using a 3-dimensional free-body diagram, as shown to the left. For instance, the front face has an area of 10cm², so the force exerted by air is 100N, pointed toward the back. The weight of the block (3.4N) and the normal force exerted by the floor are too small to show in this diagram.

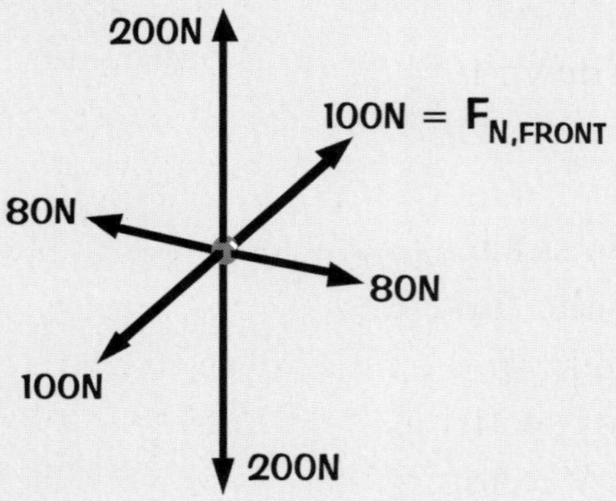

200N

100N = $F_{N,FRONT}$

80N

80N

100N

200N

You might think that there is no force on the bottom of the block, but that is impossible unless you somehow eliminate all the air from being underneath the block. One way to convince yourself of this is to imagine how hard it would be to pick up the block if there were no force pushing up due to the air. Without any air pushing up on the block, the net force due to air pressure would be 200N down, which is the weight of 20kg, or 45lb. In other words, picking up this small block of metal weighing about $3/4$lb would feel the same as picking up 45lb.

However, a suction cup is a device for which all or most of the air has been pushed out from underneath it. It is very hard to remove the suction cup from a surface because you are pulling against the force of air pressure, which is exerted on one side but not the other.

Note that to use the relationship between pressure, force, and area, the area must be flat—not necessarily horizontal, but perfectly flat. If the surface is curved, then you must consider an area small enough to be treated as being flat.

1.2 STATIC FLUIDS

The term *static* means that the fluid is at rest, or not moving. It does <u>not</u> mean that the individual molecules in the fluid are not moving. For instance, even in the absence of wind, the molecules of air at room temperature are moving with an average speed of about 1000mph. But the forces exerted by these air molecules as they collide with tables, chairs, walls, and ceilings is not air resistance, because the air as a whole is not moving relative to the objects. In other words, a static fluid exerts forces on objects it is touching, even though the molecules in it have an average velocity of zero and the fluid is "at rest".

1.2.1 The change in pressure with depth. Consider a stack of plastic plates, and focus your attention on the normal force that each exerts on the one above it. As you go down the pile, the normal force that each plate exerts on the one above it gets larger, because the weight of the pile gets larger. So, for example, the normal force exerted by the 10th plate in the pile would be equal to the weight of 9 plates.

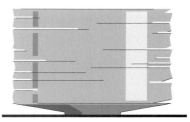

A similar effect occurs in fluids. Just as the normal force pushing up on each plate is larger on plates lower down in the pile, the pressure in a fluid is larger as you go deeper into the fluid.

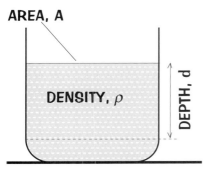

The reason is the same as with the plates. The normal force exerted by the fluid at a particular depth must be strong enough to keep the fluid above it at rest. For a container of cross-sectional area A, the volume of fluid above depth d is $V = Ad$, its mass is $m = \rho V = \rho Ad$, and its weight is $F_g = mg = \rho Adg$. Therefore, the normal force exerted by the fluid at depth d on the fluid above it must be ρAdg (i.e., the normal force balances the weight).

The pressure is the normal force divided by the (planar) area. Therefore, the pressure at depth d is ρdg.

However, we have ignored an important and common feature. Usually, there is a force due to air pushing down on the top of the fluid. This is equivalent to someone pushing down on the top of the stack of plates with an applied force F. The normal force exerted by each plate on the one above it is therefore larger by F.

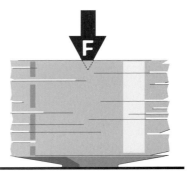

Similarly, there is a normal force of P_0A pushing down on the fluid, where P_0 is the pressure at the top of the fluid. So, the normal force pushing up on the fluid above depth d is the sum of the force pushing down on the fluid and the weight of the fluid, $P_0A + \rho Adg$. Therefore, the pressure at depth d is:

$$P(d) \;=\; P_0 + \rho g d \qquad\qquad \text{\textbf{pressure in a fluid of density } } \rho \text{ \textbf{at depth } } \textbf{\textit{d}}$$

Note that this expression does <u>not</u> depend on the shape or the cross-sectional area of the container.

1.2.2 Buoyancy. Imagine an object immersed in a fluid. Because the pressure in a fluid changes with depth, the forces exerted on different parts of the object are different. Further, because the pressure in a fluid increases with depth, the force pushing up on the bottom of the object is larger than the force pushing down on the top of the object. The horizontal forces exerted on the sides of the object balance, which means that only the forces on the top and bottom are relevant. Because the force on the bottom is larger than the force on top, there is an overall upward force. We call this force the *buoyant force*.

We can now derive the expression for the buoyant force, although we will derive it for two special cases and simply assert that it is true for all cases.

Consider a cube of density ρ' and side L hanging as shown from a string inside a fluid of density $\rho < \rho'$. Because $\rho < \rho'$, the cube would sink if the string was not there to hold it up. There are eight forces on the cube: one force exerted by the water on each face of the cube, the force of gravitation exerted by the Earth, and the tension force exerted by the string.

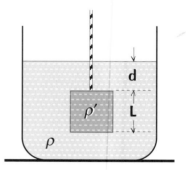

The forces due to the fluid on the four vertical faces are horizontal and have the same magnitude. They sum to zero.

The force due to fluid on the top face is equal to $(P_0 + \rho g d)L^2$, pointed down, and the force due to fluid on the bottom face is equal to $[P_0 + \rho g(d+L)]L^2$, pointed up. The weight of the cube is $\rho'gL^3$.

The buoyant force is the total force exerted by the fluid. It is the vector sum of the six forces exerted on the cube by the fluid, or

$$F_B \;=\; \left[P_0 + \rho g(d+L)\right]L^2 - \left[P_0 + \rho g d\right]L^2 \text{, pointing up}$$

Simplifying this expression, we get $F_B = \rho g L^3$. Note that this is <u>not</u> the weight of the cube, which depends on ρ'. It is the weight of a cube of fluid of density ρ. In other words, the buoyant force is the weight of the fluid that has been moved aside, or *displaced*, by the cube. In general, we write the empirical law for the buoyant force as:

$$F_B = \rho g V_{\text{displaced}}$$

empirical law for the buoyant force

where $V_{\text{displaced}}$ is the volume of fluid displaced by the object. The direction is opposite the direction of the local gravitational force.

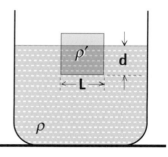

Note that $V_{\text{displaced}}$ might be smaller than the total volume of the object, such as when an object is floating. Consider a situation in which a cube of side L and density ρ' is floating in a fluid of density $\rho > \rho'$. There are now only 7 forces on the cube (there is no tension force because there is no string attached), and four of them (the horizontal forces) sum to zero, leaving three forces to focus on: the force pushing down on the top, the force pushing up on the bottom, and the weight.

The force pushing down on the top is simply $P_0 L^2$, because the top is not inside the fluid. The force pushing up on the bottom is $(P_0 + \rho g d)L^2$. The weight of the cube is $\rho' g L^3$, pointed down. The buoyant force is the sum of the two forces exerted by the fluid:

$$F_B = (P_0 + \rho g d)L^2 - P_0 L^2 = \rho g d L^2 = \rho g V_{\text{displaced}}$$

which is the same expression as before. Note that this expression does <u>not</u> depend on the shape of the floating object.

1.2.3 Buoyancy in air. Because air is a fluid, it exerts a force of buoyancy on objects immersed in it. However, because the density of air is so small compared to most everyday objects (the density of air is about 1/1000 of the density of water, or about 1 gram per liter), the pressure in air does not change very much with increasing altitude. Therefore, we often ignore this force, unless the density of the object is smaller than or close to the density of air, such as with a helium balloon.

1.2.4 Sinking vs. floating. We now have an explanation for why certain objects sink and others float: When the weight of an object ($\rho' g V$) is larger than the buoyant force ($\rho g V$), the object sinks, because the buoyant force is not large enough to support it. In other words, when the density of the object (ρ') is larger than the density of the fluid (ρ), the object sinks.

When the density of the object is smaller than the density of the fluid, part of the object must be above the surface for the buoyant force to balance the weight of the object. In other words, when the density of the object is smaller than that of the fluid, the object floats.

1.2.5 Analysis, reasoning, and problem solving with density and pressure ideas. A few examples will help you to deepen your understanding of density, pressure, the change in pressure with depth, and buoyancy.

> **A block of metal is at rest on the bottom of a container of water. What happens to the fluid pressure at the bottom of the container when you remove the block?**
>
>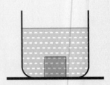
>
> **Answer.** Assuming that you remove the block completely from the fluid, the pressure at the bottom of the container decreases, because the level of the water would go down, which causes the depth of water at the bottom to be smaller than before.

A scale is useful for testing results, because you can use both pressure ideas and Newton's laws to compare predictions.

> **Is the previous result consistent with what would happen if you put the container on a scale?**
>
>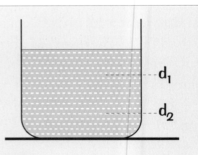
>
> **Answer.** Yes. The scale reading would get smaller, because when you remove the block, the total weight of the objects on the scale is smaller than before. This is consistent with the result that the pressure is smaller at the bottom of the container, because it means that the force exerted by fluid pressure is smaller.

> **Derive an expression for the pressure at depth d_2 in a fluid in terms of the pressure at depth d_1.**
>
> **Answer.** The pressure at depth d_1 is $P_1 = P_0 + \rho g d_1$, where ρ is the density of the fluid and P_0 is the pressure in the air above the container. The pressure at depth d_2 is $P_2 = P_0 + \rho g d_2$.
>
> Solving for P_0 in either expression, inserting the result into the other, solving for P_2, and simplifying, we get:
>
> $$P_2 = P_1 + \rho g (d_2 - d_1)$$
>
> In other words, the pressure at depth d_2 is equal to the pressure at depth d_1 plus ρg multiplied by the <u>difference</u> in depths.

Therefore, when the change in depth is positive, both the depth and the pressure are increasing, and when the change in depth is negative, both the depth and the pressure are decreasing. This expression, though equivalent to the relationship between pressure and depth derived previously, is sometimes more useful for analyzing situations and solving problems.

In the next example, we use this expression to compare the pressure at two points in a fluid.

A fluid fills a U-shaped tube as shown. One end of the tube is open to the air, and the other end is closed using a cork. Is the pressure on the bottom of the cork larger than, smaller than, or the same as atmospheric pressure?

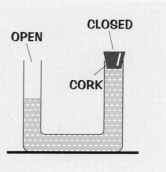

Answer. The pressure is <u>smaller</u> than the atmospheric pressure in the air. To learn why, let's focus on five points within the fluid, labeled 1 through 5 in the diagram below.

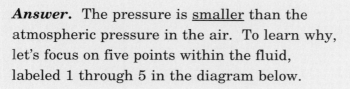

Points 1 and 4 are at the same level but on different sides of the U-tube. Points 2 and 3 are at the same level near the bottom of the tube. Point 5 is at the bottom of the cork. The pressure at point 1 is atmospheric pressure. We are interested in the pressure at point 5, so let's start at point 1 and go around to point 5.

The pressure increases from point 1 to point 2 by an amount proportional to the change in depth d, so $P_2 = P_1 + \rho g d$. Going to point 3, the pressure does not change, because the change in depth is zero, so $P_3 = P_2$. Going to point 4, the pressure decreases by an amount proportional to the change in depth, so $P_4 = P_3 - \rho g d = P_2 - \rho g d = (P_1 + \rho g d) - \rho g d = P_1$. Therefore, because point 4 is at the same level as point 1, the pressure at point 4 is equal to atmospheric pressure. Because point 5 is above point 4, the pressure at point 5 must be smaller than atmospheric pressure.

Note that in a static fluid, the change in pressure along a horizontal line is zero. Also, it was not strictly necessary to consider points 2, 3, and 4 in the fluid. Because point 5 is at a higher level than point 1, the pressure must be smaller there.

In this last example, we find that Newton's laws are still useful for answering questions.

An 18 million kilogram iceberg floats in the North Atlantic ocean. What fraction of its volume is above the surface of the water?

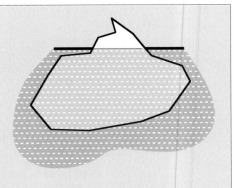

Answer. The answer does not depend on the mass or the volume of the iceberg, but only on the densities of ice and sea water. The quick answer is that ice has a density of about $0.9 \text{g}/\text{cm}^3$ and sea water has a density of about $1 \text{g}/\text{cm}^3$, so 10% of the iceberg's volume is above the surface of the ocean. Let's find out why.

The iceberg is at rest, so the net force on it must be zero. There are two non-negligible forces on the iceberg: a gravitational force exerted by the Earth and a buoyant force exerted by the water. (We are ignoring the buoyant force exerted by the air.) These forces must balance.

The gravitational force can be written mg or $(\rho_{\text{ice}} V_{\text{iceberg}})g$. The buoyant force is $(\rho_{\text{water}} V_{\text{displaced}})g$. These two forces must balance, so:

$$\left(\rho_{\text{ice}} V_{\text{iceberg}} \right) g = \left(\rho_{\text{water}} V_{\text{displaced}} \right) g$$

or:

$$\frac{V_{\text{displaced}}}{V_{\text{iceberg}}} = \frac{\rho_{\text{ice}}}{\rho_{\text{water}}} = \frac{0.9 \text{g}/\text{cm}^3}{1 \text{g}/\text{cm}^3} = 0.9 = 90\%$$

Because 90% of the volume is below the surface, 10% must be above.

This concludes the section on static fluids. Note that so far there are only two new concepts—*pressure* and *density*—and only two new principles—the change of pressure with depth and the empirical law for the buoyant force. However, these two principles are <u>not</u> independent of the ones learned before. Both are based on Newton's laws of motion and require that the fluid is at rest. In the next section, we explore fluids that are moving.

1.3 MOVING FLUIDS

Blow some air between two sheets of paper or two ping-pong balls, and the two objects move toward each other, not away from each other. Poke a hole in the side of a paper cup filled with water, and water does not just drip out, but it comes streaming out. Further, the speed at which the water comes out seems to be roughly independent of the diameter of the hole. These are examples of phenomena that can be analyzed and explained using ideas derived for *moving fluids*.

In this section, you will learn two new principles needed to understand moving fluids, and then you will apply them to a variety of situations.

1.3.1 Drawing pipes, tubes, beakers, funnels, etc. It is particularly important when learning about moving fluids and analyzing situations that you interpret the drawings correctly. These objects are three dimensional yet the drawings will usually be two dimensional. Therefore, you must try to visualize that third (missing) dimension yourself whenever you are trying to understand one of these two-dimensional representations.

Many of the situations you will encounter involve fluids moving through pipes and tubes. We usually represent them by showing a cut-away view from the side. So, for example, a garden hose would look like this:

where we often assume that the cross section is circular and that the cut-away view is done at its widest part. Note that only part of the hose might be shown.

A pipe that changes abruptly from one diameter to another is shown to the right. In this case, the diameter is 3 times as large on the left-hand side, so the cross-sectional area is 9 times as large on the left-hand side as on the right.

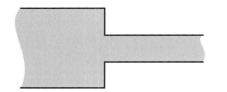

For fluid flowing in a pipe or tube, we usually represent it as shown on the left. The wiggly ends indicate that only part of the pipe is actually shown and that fluid is flowing into and out of the parts shown.

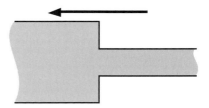

Note that we do not know which way, left or right, the fluid is flowing. Therefore, we sometimes add an arrow to the diagram to indicate the direction of flow, as shown to the right. In this case, fluid is flowing from the small pipe to the large pipe.

Beakers, glasses, funnels, etc. are also shown using cut-away views, as shown below.

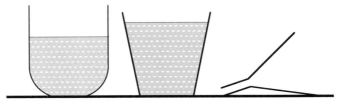

1.3.2 Conservation of mass (and its implications for fluid flow). Without a chemical or nuclear reaction, matter cannot be created or destroyed. This means that every molecule of fluid that enters a pipe must also exit the pipe. When the pipe (or tube or hose) has the same size everywhere along its length, this means that the speed of the fluid is the same everywhere also. When the pipe has a different size at different points along it, this means that the speed must be different. Let's use an example to see how this works.

Consider a pipe that has a cross-sectional area of $40cm^2$ on its left side and $10cm^2$ on its right. (The part on the left has a diameter that is two times as large as the part on the right, so its cross-sectional area is four times as large.) Water is flowing left-to-right at a rate of $40g/s$. In other words, conservation of mass requires that every second, 40 grams of water enter the pipe on the left, and 40 grams of water leave the pipe on the right.

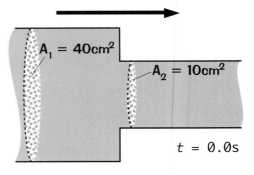

But what does this have to do with the speeds of the water in different parts of the pipe? The density of water is roughly constant in all conditions (i.e., varying temperature and pressure), with a value of $1g/cm^3$. This means that the volume of water entering and leaving the pipe every second is $40cm^3$. Assuming that the disks in the diagram above represent a layer of water molecules in the pipe at a particular instant, we can look at the same molecules of water in the pipe one second later, as shown on the left.

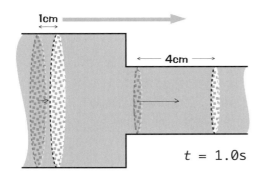

The water on the left side of the pipe must move to the right to make room for the $40cm^3$ of water entering the pipe every second. Because the cross-sectional area is $40cm^2$, the disk of water moves 1cm to the right, which means that the water in the left side of the pipe has a speed of $1cm/s$. Likewise, the water in the right side of the pipe must move to the right to make room for the $40cm^3$ of water entering it. Therefore, the disk of water moves 4cm every second, which means that the water in the right side has a speed of $4cm/s$.

In general, the speed of the fluid in one part of a pipe is related to the speed in another part according to their relative cross-sectional areas. The larger the area, the smaller the speed. In particular, conservation of mass requires that:

$$\rho_1 A_1 v_1 \;=\; \rho_2 A_2 v_2 \qquad\qquad \textbf{fluid flow in a pipe}$$

Note that the units of $\rho A v$ are grams per second, and that this quantity is the rate at which fluid is flowing through the pipe. In most situations the density of the fluid does not change with position, so the relation becomes simply $A_1 v_1 = A_2 v_2$. You will find that this is a very useful relationship for analysis and problem solving.

1.3.3 Bernoulli's principle.

As a fluid moves through a pipe or tube, the pressure changes depending on how fast the fluid is moving or what height the pipe or tube is raised or lowered to. The relationship is called *Bernoulli's Principle*, and it is written mathematically as:

$$P_1 - P_2 \;=\; \rho g\!\left(y_2 - y_1\right) + \tfrac{1}{2}\rho\!\left(v_2{}^2 - v_1{}^2\right) \qquad\qquad \textbf{Bernoulli's Principle}$$

where P_n is the pressure in the fluid at point n, ρ is the density of the fluid, y_n is the y-coordinate of the fluid at point n, and v_n is the speed of the fluid at point n. We are assuming that the density is constant.

The y-dependent part of Bernoulli's principle is similar to the expression we used previously for a static fluid. The only difference is that Bernoulli's principle is written in terms of the height y, whereas the other was written in terms of the depth d. In either case, when the fluid is at rest, the speed v is zero, and the pressure P increases with depth.

The speed-dependent part of Bernoulli's principle needs more explaining. You might think that when a pipe widens, the pressure should decrease, because the pipe is no longer squeezing the fluid. Or you might think that when a pipe gets very small, the pressure should increase, again because the pipe is squeezing the fluid inside the small part. Actually, the opposite is true: When a pipe widens, the pressure increases and when a pipe narrows, the pressure decreases.

By way of example, let's focus on the first of these two possibilities: Fluid flows from a large pipe to a small pipe as shown to the right. The fluid is moving faster on the right than on the left, which means that positive work is done on the fluid during the transition region in the middle. The sequence of drawings on the next page shows the transition of the fluid.

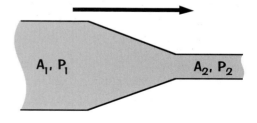

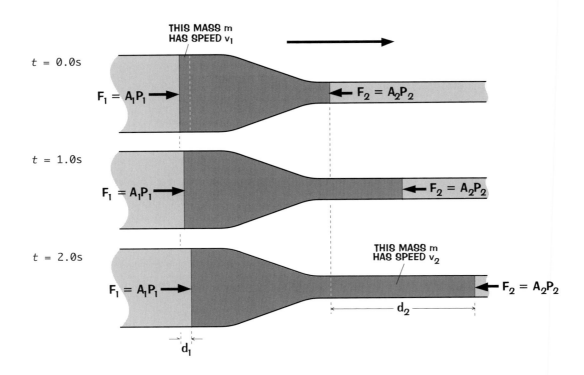

At each of the three instants shown, the amount of fluid shown in dark gray is the same. The fluid is moving faster on the right side, so the right edge of the fluid moves farther during each interval. Here is a quick derivation of the speed-dependent part of Bernoulli's principle:

Step	Relationship	Reason / assumption
1	$W_{\text{net}} = \Delta KE_{\text{tot}}$	Work–Kinetic Energy theorem relates the net work done on something to the change in its total kinetic energy.
2	$W_{\text{net}} = F_1 d_1 - F_2 d_2$	Definitions of work and net work. The fluid on the far left is doing positive work $F_1 d_1$ on the fluid in the middle, and the fluid on the right is doing negative work $-F_2 d_2$ on the fluid in the middle. The walls of the pipe do no work on the fluid.
3	$F_1 = A_1 P_1;\; F_2 = A_2 P_2$	Definition of force due to a fluid under pressure.
4	$\Delta KE_{\text{tot}} = \tfrac{1}{2} m\left(v_2{}^2 - v_1{}^2\right)$	Definition of kinetic energy. m is the mass of fluid in volumes $A_1 d_1$ and $A_2 d_2$ (see diagram).
5	$m = \rho A_1 d_1 = \rho A_2 d_2$	Definitions of density and volume. We assume that the density of the fluid does not change. Note that $A_1 d_1 = A_2 d_2$, which means that $W_{\text{net}} = (P_1 - P_2)A_1 d_1$
6	$P_1 - P_2 = \tfrac{1}{2}\rho\left(v_2{}^2 - v_1{}^2\right)$	Insert relationships from steps 2–5 into the relationship in step 1 and simplify.

So, for example, when $v_2 > v_1$, the right-hand side is positive, which means that the left-hand side must be positive as well. Therefore, the pressure is smaller, i.e., $P_2 < P_1$.

1.3.4 Conditions under which Bernoulli's principle is valid. It is important to recognize that Bernoulli's principle is really a statement of energy conservation. For the height-dependent part, if the speed does not change, it says that the work done on a sample of fluid by the fluid on either side of it is equal to the change in the sample's gravitational potential energy. For the speed-dependent part, if the height does not change, it says that the work done on the sample is equal to the change in its kinetic energy. So, in general, because the sides of the pipe do no work, the total work done on the sample is equal to the change in its total energy.

As such, there are four main assumptions made about the fluid and its flow to derive Bernoulli's principle:

1. At any particular horizontal position along a pipe or tube, the pressure and velocity must be constant in time. We refer to this as being *steady state*.

2. Also at any particular horizontal position along a pipe or tube, the pressure and velocity must be uniform. We refer to this as *laminar* or *streamline* flow. For instance, if water from a small pipe is flowing into a much larger pipe, we might expect that the water would not be flowing smoothly near the opening. There might even be some swirling of water. This would be called *turbulent* or *chaotic*, and Bernoulli's principle could not be applied.

3. The density must be independent of pressure, otherwise the volume of the sample of fluid would change as it moved through the pipe and make the derivation invalid. We refer to these fluids as *incompressible*.

4. There must be no dissipation of energy from the macroscopic realm (kinetic and gravitational potential) to the microscopic realm by friction-like forces between the fluid molecules. We call this type of fluid *non-viscous* or say that it has very little *viscosity*. Oil is "thicker" than water, because it is more viscous.

In the following two sections we present extended examples of how to apply Bernoulli's principle.

1.3.5 Applications of Bernoulli's principle. A series of five holes are drilled into the side of a large container filled with water as shown. (We choose the container to be large so that we can assume that the level of the water does not change very quickly even though water is leaking out of it.) What can we say about the water leaving the holes? Will the water just dribble out, or will it shoot out quickly? How quickly? How far will it project? Will the way the water leaves depend on which hole it leaves from? How will the size of the hole affect the speed of the exiting water?

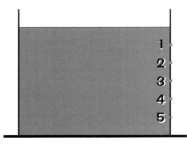

These are all answerable questions, but first we need to understand how a single hole works. So let's focus on one of the holes and analyze it first, then apply what we have learned to the situation above.

We assume simply that we have a small hole in the side of a container. The pressure is P inside the container far to the left of the hole, and the fluid is not moving inside the container.

Because the fluid is unconstrained (by a pipe, for example) outside the hole, the pressure in it is P_{atm}. Because P is larger than P_{atm}, there is a net force on the fluid near the hole causing it to accelerate. Assuming the flow is steady-state, we will use Bernoulli's principle to find the speed of the fluid outside the container.

Therefore, assuming steady-state, streamline flow through the hole, $P - P_{atm} = {}^{1}\!/_{2}\rho v^{2}$, where v is the speed of the fluid just outside the hole. Solving for v, we get, $v = \sqrt{2(P - P_{atm})/\rho}$. This means that the larger the difference in pressures, the larger the speed. Also, it would appear that the smaller the density, the larger the speed. However, we will see that this is not always the case, especially when P depends upon ρ.

Now we can return to the original situation of five holes drilled into the side of a container. Assuming that the first hole is drilled a distance d below the surface of the water, and that each subsequent hole is drilled a distance d below the one above it, we can determine how quickly the water exits each of the holes. The table below summarizes the results.

Hole	Depth of hole	Pressure inside hole	Speed outside hole
1	d	$P_{atm} + \rho g d$	$\sqrt{gd}$
2	$2d$	$P_{atm} + 2\rho g d$	$\sqrt{2gd}$
3	$3d$	$P_{atm} + 3\rho g d$	$\sqrt{3gd}$
4	$4d$	$P_{atm} + 4\rho g d$	$\sqrt{4gd}$
5	$5d$	$P_{atm} + 5\rho g d$	$\sqrt{5gd}$

Note that for this situation the speed outside each hole does not depend on the density of the fluid. This is not the general case, but occurs only because of the algebraic form for the pressure inside the hole (i.e., column 3 in the table above). Also, the speed is independent of the size of the hole, because we have not used this information to derive our expressions. Finally, the table indicates that the speed of the water coming out of the top hole is smallest and the speed of the water coming out of the bottom hole is the largest.

But which hole will cause water to shoot the farthest? In other words, if the container is on the floor or a table, which water spout will land the farthest from the container?

To answer this question, you must recall your kinematics. For a typical parabolic trajectory of an object thrown horizontally, the distance along the ground is related to the initial speed and initial height according to $D = v\Delta t = v\sqrt{2H/g}$, where Δt is the time it takes for the object to reach the ground.

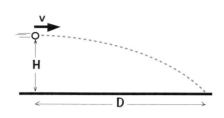

So, assuming that the bottom hole is height d above the ground and that the water molecules follow a typical trajectory, we get the following table of distances.

Hole	Height of hole	Speed outside hole	Where the water lands
1	$5d$	$\sqrt{gd}$	$\sqrt{10}\cdot d \approx 3.2d$
2	$4d$	$\sqrt{2gd}$	$\sqrt{16}\cdot d = 4d$
3	$3d$	$\sqrt{3gd}$	$\sqrt{18}\cdot d \approx 4.2d$
4	$2d$	$\sqrt{4gd}$	$\sqrt{16}\cdot d = 4d$
5	d	$\sqrt{5gd}$	$\sqrt{10}\cdot d \approx 3.2d$

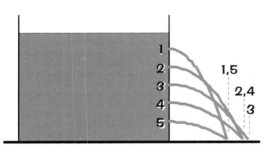

So, although the bottom hole produces water with the largest speed, the middle hole produces water that lands the farthest from the container. And water coming out of holes the same distance above and below the middle hole produce water that lands at the same point. A diagram is shown to the left.

1.3.6 Siphons. As a final application of Bernoulli's principle, we will investigate the siphon. This is a good context because it involves many different ideas of moving fluids: not only Bernoulli's principle, but conservation of mass, Newton's laws, and conservation of energy.

The siphon is a good situation to study for another reason. It requires us to be strategic in the way we analyze it. In other words, the order in which the analysis is done is critical. The wrong approach will cause you to get all tangled up in relationships or feel like you are going around in circles. Remember: if you do not have enough information to determine something, look for another principle that you might use, such as conservation of mass.

A typical siphon is shown below. Fluid enters the tube at point 2 and exits at point 6. Other points along the path of the fluid are indicated as well. We will use these points throughout our analysis and discussion.

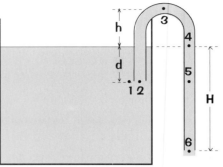

What do we know? We assume that fluid is <u>not</u> moving at point 1 (just outside the tube in the tank), but it <u>is</u> moving at point 2. How is this possible? Just as in the case of the hole in the side of the cup, there is a rapid acceleration of fluid as it enters the tube, which is associated with a drop in pressure at point 2 (compared to just outside the tube at point 1).

We know that the fluid is moving with the same speed (call it v) at points 2, 3, 4, 5 and 6. You might think that the fluid is slowing down on its way up and speeding up on its way back down again, but this is impossible because the tube diameter is the same everywhere. If the speed of the fluid were changing, the mass could not be conserved. We are assuming that the density of the fluid is constant, so the speed inside the tube must be constant as well.

We also know that the pressure at point 6 is $P_6 = P_{atm} = 10 \text{N}/\text{cm}^2$, because that is where the fluid exits the tube and the fluid there is exposed to the air.

What else do we know? We know that the pressure at point 1 depends on the depth of the fluid at that point (call it depth d). Mathematically, $P_1 = P_{atm} + \rho g d$.

What do we <u>not</u> know? We do not know the pressures inside the tube at points 2, 3, 4, and 5, and we do not know the speed v of the fluid inside the tube.

To find these we first recognize that if we assume that the behavior is steady-state, then we can apply Bernoulli's principle. Therefore, we can relate the pressure and speed at any point in the fluid (tube <u>and</u> tank) to the speed and pressure at any other point. We <u>choose</u> to relate points 1 and 6, because then the only unknown is the speed v. (This is what we mean by taking a strategic approach.)

Bernoulli's principle:	$P_a - P_b = \rho g(y_b - y_a) + \tfrac{1}{2}\rho(v_b{}^2 - v_a{}^2)$
Apply to points 1 and 6:	$P_1 - P_6 = \rho g(-H - (-d)) + \tfrac{1}{2}\rho v^2$
Pressure at point 1:	$P_1 = P_{atm} + \rho g d$
Pressure at point 6:	$P_6 = P_{atm}$
Insert and simplify:	$v = \sqrt{2gH}$

Note that the speed does not depend on d or h. It depends only on how far the end of the tube <u>outside</u> the tank is below the surface of the fluid in the tank. So, for instance, when $H = 20$cm, $v = 2$m/s.

What happens when the end of the tube (point 6) is above the beginning of the tube (point 2)? In particular, will the siphon continue to function? Yes, as long as $H > 0$. In other words, the end of the siphon does not need to be below the beginning of the tube, but it does need to be below the surface of the water.

What is the pressure at each of the labeled points along the tube? Here is a table showing the speed and pressure at all 6 points, using values of $g = 10$N/kg, $\rho = \rho_{water} = 1$g/cm^3 = 1000kg/m^3, $h = 10$cm, $d = 15$cm, and $H = 20$cm. (Keep in mind that atmospheric pressure is about 10N/cm^2.)

Point	Speed of fluid (m/s)	Height of fluid relative to surface of the water (cm)	Height of fluid relative to the end of the tube, point 6 (cm)	Mathematical expression for the pressure	Pressure (N/cm^2)
1	0	−15	5	$P_{atm} + \rho g d$	10.15
2	2	−15	5	$P_{atm} - \rho g(H - d)$	9.95
3	2	10	30	$P_{atm} - \rho g(H + h)$	9.7
4	2	0	20	$P_{atm} - \rho g H$	9.8
5	2	−15	5	$P_{atm} - \rho g(H - d)$	9.95
6	2	−20	0	P_{atm}	10

Note that the smallest pressure is at point 3, the topmost point of the tube. Since the pressure there is smaller than atmospheric pressure, this means that if h is large enough, the siphon will not work. Specifically, because the pressure in the tube must always be positive, the largest h for a siphon is $P_{atm}/\rho g = 10$ meters.

Would a siphon work on the Moon? Maybe! The value of g there is smaller, but that is not really the limiting factor. The problem is that there is no air pressure on the Moon. This means that those points at which the pressure is less than 10N/cm^2 on the Earth would have a negative pressure on the Moon, which is impossible. For points 2, 4, and 5, we can solve this problem by reducing H to a very small value. But at point 3—the topmost point in the fluid— we would still have a negative pressure, so it would be impossible to get the fluid to rise inside the tube. However, if the siphon were inside a pressurized dome on the Moon (for example) then the siphon would work.

1.3.7 Limitations of Bernoulli's principle. It is easy to find situations that violate Bernoulli's principle. For instance, in the case in which 5 holes were poked in the side of a cup, we derived an expression for the speed at which the water exits the hole. This expression was independent of the size of the hole. This is clearly false, because if the hole is too small, for example, water comes out in droplets rather than in a steady stream. (This is caused by surface tension.) Also, if the hole is too big, water simply pours out.

Other limitations are related to the other assumptions made to derive Bernoulli's principle. For instance, if there is a barrier or structure that the fluid must go around or past, then it might become difficult to maintain smooth, steady-state flow. Some fluids tend to adhere to walls, which means that the speed of the fluid would not be uniform across the cross section of the pipe, hose, or tube. There can be frictional effects between the fluid and the walls as well. Finally, if the fluid level in a tank is changing, then systems such as the siphon become more complicated to analyze, because the pressure at any particular point is changing as the height of the fluid is changing.

In spite of all these potential limitations, Bernoulli's principle can be applied in a wide variety of situations to make good approximations about the behavior of moving fluids.

We cannot know the behavior of individual atoms and molecules in a fluid, and you might think that because a fluid is not rigid, it might be difficult to apply Newton's laws and conservation laws, but remarkably, when analyzed as an aggregate system, the details average out, and we get the results derived so far.

In this chapter, you have learned about two new concepts—*pressure* and *density*—and four new principles involving them. The first two new principles are understood using Newton's laws: the change of pressure with depth and the empirical law for the buoyant force are both derived by assuming simply that the net force on a sample of fluid or on an object immersed in a fluid is zero.

The third new principle is a new conservation law: conservation of mass, which leads to a very useful relationship for fluid flow in different parts of a pipe. Because the flow rate (e.g., in kg/s) must be the same everywhere in a pipe or tube, the speed of an incompressible fluid is inversely proportional to the cross-sectional area of the pipe. And the fourth new principle is understood using conservation of energy: Bernoulli's principle relates the pressure in a fluid with its height and speed. For a sample of fluid flowing in a pipe of changing height and cross section, the total work done on the sample by external forces is equal to the change in its kinetic and gravitational potential energies.

In the next chapter, you will study the concepts of *heat*, *temperature*, and *entropy*.

HEAT, TEMPERATURE, AND ENTROPY

There are many ways to change the energy of an object or a system. We can change its potential energy, or we can change its kinetic energy. These changes can be done in a number of ways. You have learned about elastic and gravitational potential energy. We can also change an object's kinetic energy by changing either its speed or its rate of spinning. In the large majority of situations you have studied so far, changes in energy have been macroscopic, meaning large scale, as opposed to microscopic, or small scale.

We can also change how energy is distributed in a system. For instance, take as a system the atmosphere of the Earth. As an electrical storm moves from one location to another, energy also moves with it because the storm has a high concentration of potential and kinetic energies. But again, most of the situations you have studied so far involve large-scale changes in the distribution of energy.

In this chapter, we will study small-scale changes in energy and the distribution of energy. Every macroscopic object is actually a system of microscopic objects. For instance, you can think of a solid as a collection of rigid objects interconnected by springs. The rigid objects represent the atoms and molecules of the solid, and the springs represent the interactions that each has with its neighbors. Imagine a bottle of cold milk sitting on a table. Its macroscopic kinetic energy is constant because its speed is not changing. Its macroscopic potential energy is constant because its position is not changing. However, air molecules are interacting with the bottle, adding energy to the outermost layer of molecules. These molecules in turn interact with molecules deeper in the bottle. Microscopic energy flows from the air in the room to the bottle, and eventually to the cold milk.

In this chapter, we will show you how to use force, momentum, and energy ideas to understand microscopic changes in systems. We will also introduce three new concepts—*heat*, *temperature*, and *entropy*—which will help to organize and explain the changes.

2.1 HEAT AND TEMPERATURE

In everyday language we do not use the term *heat* very precisely. We sometimes use the term to refer to a form of energy and sometimes we use the term to describe the transfer of energy. Our body is constantly engaging in a variety of chemical processes that generate excess energy usually called *heat*. We have a fairly narrow comfortable range of body temperatures and regulate our environment to maintain our temperature to be within that range. Under normal circumstances this regulation requires that we transfer energy from our bodies to the environment at a significant rate.

Our human sense of temperature is also not very precise. The reason is that our senses are highly sensitive to the <u>transfer</u> of energy. Thus, we feel cold when we lose energy too quickly and we feel hot when we do not lose thermal energy quickly enough. This is why metal, which is a good thermal energy conductor (just as it is a good electrical conductor), feels cool to the touch even when it is at room temperature. Even though the air and the metal are both at room temperature, energy is transferred from your hand to the metal more quickly than to the air, so the metal feels cooler. This is also why blowing through a straw at your hand feels cool, but blowing through the straw at a thermometer will raise its temperature above room temperature. Your breath is actually warmer than your hand, but when you blow on your hand, the moving air can carry energy away, so it actually cools your hand slightly. Blowing on a thermometer adds energy, which raises its temperature.

As we explore the ideas of *heat* and *temperature*, keep in mind that Newton's laws and conservation of momentum and energy still apply. The difficulty is applying these physics principles to uncountably large numbers of atoms and molecules. The trick will be that by focusing on average values of different quantities, we can avoid the need to know what every particle is doing.

2.1.1 Temperature. Most of us have some experience with temperature. In everyday usage, temperature is simply the reading on a thermometer. But even this simple definition requires a deeper physical principle:

THE PRINCIPLE OF THERMAL EQUILIBRIUM

When two systems are in contact, they will exchange energy until they are at the same temperature.

The reading on a thermometer is really the temperature <u>of the thermometer</u>. However, if we assume that the thermometer is in thermal equilibrium with its surroundings, then the reading is also the temperature of the surroundings.

A related idea is that certain materials, such as STYROFOAM, inhibit the flow of energy from one system to another and therefore can be used to *thermally isolate* or *thermally insulate* one system from another. This procedure is especially useful when we want to study a system that is not at room temperature or when we want to study a system with constant energy.

The standard MKS unit of temperature is °C (degrees Centigrade) or K (Kelvin). The melting point of water is 0°C and its boiling point is 100°C. The Kelvin scale will be defined in a later section.

2.1.2 Effects of mixing. When two systems are put into thermal contact, if one of the systems is at a higher temperature than the other, it will transfer energy to the other until the two systems are at the same temperature. But what will that final temperature be? We will investigate this question in three contexts: (1) the same materials and amounts; (2) the same materials but different amounts of material; and (3) different materials.

EQUAL AMOUNTS OF THE SAME MATERIAL

Let's start with 400g of water at 30°C and 400g of water at 54°C. Each is in a STYROFOAM container to minimize the amount of energy exchanged with the environment, for instance, the air in the room. Further, we will assume that <u>no</u> energy is exchanged with the environment. The situation is shown below.

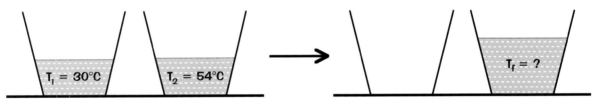

One possible prediction for the final temperature is the average of the two initial temperatures, $\frac{1}{2}(T_1 + T_2) = \frac{1}{2}(30°C + 54°C) = 42°C$. Experimentally, this turns out to be correct, but the reason is more complicated than you might think. The final temperature is the average of the initial temperatures due to three factors: (1) the materials are the same type, in this case, water; (2) the amounts of material are the same, in this case, 400g; and (3) the change in temperature is directly proportional to the amount of energy transferred.

The changes in energy are related to conservation of energy. Because energy is conserved, the amount of energy gained by the first cup of water must be equal to the amount of energy given up by the second cup of water. Because the change in temperature is proportional to the amount of energy transferred, for identical amounts of water, the temperature rise of the one must be equal to the temperature drop of the second. In this case, one-half of the water goes from a temperature of 30°C to 42°C, a rise of 12°C. The other half of the water goes from 54°C to 42°C, a drop of 12°C.

DIFFERENT AMOUNTS OF THE SAME MATERIAL

When the amounts of material are different, the final temperature is not the average of the initial temperatures. For instance, let's start with 800g of water at 30° (that is, twice as much as before) and 400g of water at 54°C (that is, the same amount as before). Because there is twice as much water at 30°C, its change in temperature will only be half as much as the water at 54°C, because the energy it gains from the other water is distributed over twice as much mass. Therefore, we can deduce that the final temperature of the mixture is 38°C, because then the 800g at 30°C experiences a temperature rise of 8°C and the 400g at 52°C experiences a temperature drop of 16°C. (Algebraically, $2(T - 30°C) = 54°C - T$ is solved by $T = 38°C$.)

We can also arrive at the same final temperature by imagining a sequence in which only 400g of the 800g of water at one temperature is mixed with the 400g at a different temperature. Start by mixing 400g of the water at 30°C into the water at 54°C. This is the same process as above, so we know the result: We are left with 400g of water at 30°C (unmixed) and 800g of water at 42°C (mixed), as indicated in the diagram below.

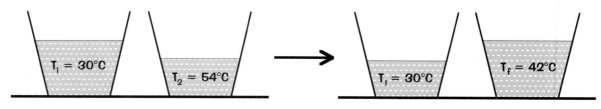

When the other 400g of water at 30°C is mixed in, the final temperature will be smaller than 42°C. Therefore, the result will not be the average, but a temperature closer to the temperature of the material of which there is more.

As this process is repeated, the temperatures of the two samples become closer and closer to each other, eventually reaching a final, common temperature of 38°C as before. The table to the right shows the results of four successive mixings as well as the final result (labeled ∞).

| | CUP 1 | | CUP 2 | | |
Step	Mass (g)	Temp. (°C)	Mass (g)	Temp. (°C)	Diagram
0	800	30	400	54	30°C 54°C
1	400	30	800	42	30°C 42°C
2	800	36	400	42	36°C 42°C
3	400	36	800	39	36°C 39°C
4	800	37½	400	39	37½°C 39°C
∞	400	38	800	38	38°C 38°C

The type of material affects the result as well. If 400g of water at 30°C is mixed with 400g of aluminum at 54°C, we do not expect the result to be the same as when the 30°C water is mixed with 400g of water at 54°C. The reason is that it takes less energy to change the temperature of aluminum by 1°C than it does to change the temperature of water by 1°C. In particular, it takes about 5 times as much energy to change the temperature of water, which means that the change in temperature of the aluminum is about 5 times the change in temperature of the water. Therefore, the final temperature of the mixture is about 34°C. In other words, even though the energy gained by the water is exactly equal to the energy lost by the aluminum, the water temperature rises 4°C and the aluminum temperature falls 20°C.

2.1.3 Specific heat. To take into account the differences in how materials respond to gains or losses in energy, we define the *specific heat*. It is the amount of energy needed to change the temperature of 1 gram of a material by one degree Centigrade. Although the specific heat generally depends on the temperature, it remains roughly constant for a wide range of temperatures and pressures. Some values of the specific heat are shown to the right for everyday temperatures and pressures. Note that ice and steam have different specific heats than liquid water. The value given in the table is for water between 0°C and 100°C at atmospheric pressure.

	SPECIFIC HEAT	
Material	**J/g·°C**	**cal/g·°C**
Aluminum	0.900	0.215
Copper	0.387	0.0924
Water	4.186	1.000

Note that the last column is given in terms of the *calorie*. This is a unit of energy often used in this context because the specific heat of water is 1cal/g·°C. However, this is <u>not</u> the same as the unit of energy used in nutrition and food labeling. That is called the *Calorie* (with a capital "C"), but it is really a kilocalorie; that is, 1kcal = 1000cal = 1Cal.

Note also that 1cal is the same amount of energy as about 4J. This means that it takes about the same amount of energy to change the temperature of 1g of water by 1°C (i.e., 1cal) as it takes to raise 400g (about 1 pound) by 1m (i.e., $mg\Delta y \approx 4J$).

In terms of the specific heat, assuming that the specific heat does not change with varying temperature, the change in energy of a material is:

$$\Delta E = mc\Delta T$$

change in energy of a material whose specific heat does not depend on temperature

where m is the mass of the material, c is its specific heat, and ΔT is its change in temperature.

Because energy is conserved, when two objects are mixed, we can predict the final temperature, as long as we know enough about the situation.

> **600g of copper wire at 80°C is put into 200g of water at 20°C. What is the final temperature of the copper and water?**
>
> *Answer.* Assuming that energy is conserved and that no energy is transferred to the air, the energy gained by the water must be equal to the energy lost by the copper wire. Mathematically, $m_w c_w (T_f - 20°C)$ is equal to $m_c c_c (80°C - T_f)$. Everything but T_f is known, so we can solve for it. The result is 33°C.

We can check our result by computing the energy gained by the water and the energy lost by the copper and making sure they are equal:

Energy gained by the water:

$$
\begin{aligned}
\Delta E_{water} &= m_w c_w \Delta T_w \\
&= 200g \times 1 cal/g{\cdot}°C \times 13°C \\
&= 2600 cal
\end{aligned}
$$

Energy lost by the copper:

$$
\begin{aligned}
\Delta E_{copper} &= m_c c_c \Delta T_c \\
&= 600g \times 0.0924 cal/g{\cdot}°C \times (-47°C) \\
&= -2606 cal
\end{aligned}
$$

These amounts are about equal, so we can say with confidence that the final temperature is about 33°C.

2.1.4 Microscopic vs. macroscopic work. There are two ways that one system can do work on another system. The first is microscopically, such as when two systems at different temperatures are mixed. There is a transfer of microscopic energy, which we call *heat*.

> **HEAT (or microscopic work)**
>
> **The amount of energy transferred from one system to another due to a temperature difference between them.**

The systems are assumed to be in thermal contact, which allows the atoms and molecules in one system to do work on the atoms and molecules in the system it is touching. When the two systems are in equilibrium, the temperatures of the two systems are the same, and no more energy is transferred.

Note that heat is not an attribute of a system but of a process. A system does not "have heat". Instead, when a system loses microscopic energy, we say that "heat flows" from the system or that "energy is transferred" to another system. In this way, heat is like work and impulse, which are used to describe <u>changes</u> in the properties of a system.

Macroscopic work is the type we studied in Book 3. When you lift a book or throw a ball or pull a wagon, you are doing macroscopic work, and the definition is the same as before.

> **WORK (or macroscopic work)**
>
> **The amount of energy transferred to or from a system by exerting a force through a displacement.**

This means that there are two ways of changing the energy of a system: by doing microscopic work or by doing macroscopic work. Both of these are due to external forces.

$$\Delta E = W_{\text{micro}} + W_{\text{macro}} \qquad \text{change in energy of a system}$$

Note that this is simply a restatement of the Work–Energy Theorem ($W_{\text{ext}} = \Delta E_{\text{total}}$).

As stated earlier, we generally refer to the microscopic work as the heat given to a system. The symbol used for the heat given is Q. When heat is removed from the system, Q is negative.

Even though it can be confusing, it is traditional to refer to the macroscopic work simply as the work done on the system, and the symbol used for it is W. When the macroscopic work is positive, energy is added to the system, and when W is negative, energy is removed from the system.

We now can rewrite the equation above as:

$$\Delta E = Q + W \qquad \text{1st law of thermodynamics}$$

This is called the *First Law of Thermodynamics*. Although the full meanings of these ideas are now somewhat hidden within the symbols chosen to represent them, try to keep foremost in your mind that Q is the microscopic work done on a system and W is the macroscopic work done on the system. This will help you greatly when you analyze systems and solve problems. Remember also that even though we call this statement the 1st law of thermodynamics, it is really just a restatement of conservation of energy.

2.2 RELATING THERMAL MOTION AND TEMPERATURE

Our goal in this chapter is to be able to predict the behavior of interacting systems using thermodynamic quantities such as *heat* and *temperature*. We have already used conservation of energy to make a number of predictions about mixing, but those situations only involve microscopic changes. We would like to consider macroscopic changes as well. In this section, we will derive the relationships needed to analyze a wider variety of situations. We will use the *Perfect Gas Law*, because it is the only model which gives an exact result.

2.2.1 Perfect (or Ideal) Gas Law. You may have seen the Perfect Gas Law (or the Ideal Gas Law) in prior courses. It is a relationship based on experimental observations of the behavior of dilute gases. The relationship is:

$$\frac{PV}{n} = RT + \text{constant}$$ **Perfect Gas Law**

where P is the pressure of the gas, V is its volume, n is the number of moles of gas, R is the Universal Gas Constant ($8.314 \text{J/mole·}°C = 1.9872 \text{cal/mole·}°C$), and T is the temperature measured using any linear scale, such as Centigrade or Fahrenheit. The constant depends on which scale for temperature you use. Remarkably, this relationship is true for any gas, as long as its density is small.

2.2.2 The Kelvin temperature scale. There are two commonly used temperature scales, the Fahrenheit scale and the Centigrade scale. As you may already know these scales are defined by assigning specific numerical values for the freezing and boiling points of pure water, and by so doing dividing the scale into some particular number of intervals. For example, the Centigrade scale assigns 0 to the freezing point and 100 to the boiling point (of water), while the Fahrenheit scale assigns 32 to the freezing point and 212 to the boiling point (of water).

The *Kelvin* temperature scale is defined using a gas thermometer. Because gases (especially dilute gases) obey the Perfect Gas Law, when the volume and number of moles of gas are constant, pressure vs. temperature is a straight line, as shown by the solid line in the graph to the right.

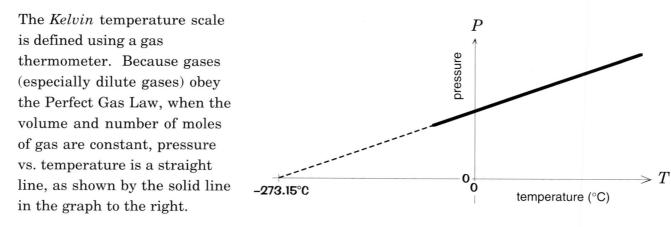

If we extend the straight line to smaller and smaller temperatures and pressures, we reach a limit for how cold the gas can be. This occurs at −273.15°C, which is often referred to as *absolute zero*, because this is the zero point of the Kelvin temperature scale. Also, a change of one degree on the Kelvin scale is the same as that for the Centigrade scale, so the relationship between the temperatures on the two scales is given by:

$$T_K = T_C + 273.15 \qquad \text{conversion from Centigrade to Kelvin temperature}$$

The "constant" in the Perfect Gas Law is zero for the Kelvin temperature scale, so we can rewrite the Perfect Gas Law to be:

$$\frac{PV}{n} = RT_K \qquad \text{Perfect Gas Law using the Kelvin temperature scale}$$

or in its more familiar form:

$$PV = nRT_K \qquad \text{Perfect Gas Law using the Kelvin temperature scale}$$

where now the temperature <u>must</u> be measured using the Kelvin scale.

2.2.3 Energy in a perfect gas at temperature T_K. Imagine a cube of side d, with a single gas particle in it. Assume that the gas particle has mass m and that it is initially moving to the right as shown with speed v_x. Assume also that the speed of the gas particle is so large that it hits the sides of the box many times every second.

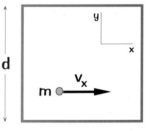

Each time a gas particle hits a wall or other surface, it exerts a (relatively) large normal force for a very short period of time. Because the particle is moving so rapidly, there is a well defined pressure on the walls of the box, which results from the interactions of the gas particle with the wall. (See section 1.1.5 beginning on page R5 for a definition of pressure.) The wall also exerts a force, which delivers the impulse needed to change the gas particle's momentum. The impulse delivered by, for instance, the left wall is equal to the change in the particle's momentum, $J = \Delta p = 2mv_x$ every time it hits the wall. The time between hits is the time it takes the particle to go a distance $2d$: $\Delta t = 2d/v_x$. So, every Δt, the wall exerts a force that changes the momentum of the particle by $2mv_x$. Therefore, from the definition of impulse, we know that the average force exerted by the wall is $F_{ave} = J/\Delta t = mv_x^2/d$. The pressure P depends on the area of the wall. The pressure exerted on the left and right walls is $P = F_{ave}/d^2 = mv_x^2/d^3$. This sequence of steps is shown in the figure on the next page.

Definition of pressure:	$P = F_{\text{ave}} / \text{area of wall} = F_{\text{ave}} / d^2$
Definition of impulse:	$J = F_{\text{ave}} \Delta t$ — so — $F_{\text{ave}} = J / \Delta t$
Impulse–momentum theorem:	$J = \Delta p$
Definition of momentum:	$\Delta p = 2mv_x$ each time the particle hits the wall
Definition of velocity:	$v_x = 2d / \Delta t$ — so — $\Delta t = 2d / v_x$

Inserting these relationships and simplifying, we get:

$$P = \frac{F_{\text{ave}}}{d^2} = \frac{mv_x^2}{d^3}$$

**pressure on the left and right walls
of the box due to <u>one</u> gas particle**

When the motion of the gas particle is not limited only to the x-direction, the pressure on the left or right wall of the box still depends <u>only</u> on the x-component of velocity v_x.

When there are many particles inside the box, we simply add the forces together to get the total force exerted by all the particles. Still, the pressure on the left or right wall of the box depends only on the x-components of the velocities of all the particles in the box:

$$P = \frac{mv_{1x}^2 + mv_{2x}^2 + \ldots + mv_{Nx}^2}{d^3}$$

**pressure on the left and right walls
of the box due to <u>many</u> gas particles**

where N is the total number of gas particles in the box, and v_{1x} is the x-component of the first gas particle, v_{2x} is the x-component of the second gas particle, etc.

The numerator on the right-hand side above <u>looks</u> like the total kinetic energy, but not quite. First, it is missing a factor of $1/2$. Second, it is missing contributions from the y- and z-components of velocity. (Keep in mind that the box is three-dimensional.) We can say, however, that the total kinetic energy has equal contributions due to components in the x-, y-, and z-directions. Therefore, the numerator above is equal to $2/3 E_{K,\text{total}}$.

The denominator on the right-hand side is the volume of the box, so the relationship may be rearranged to get $PV = 2/3 E_{K,\text{total}}$. Now, using the Perfect Gas Law, we can relate the total kinetic energy in a perfect gas to the temperature of the gas:

$$E_{K,\text{total}} = \frac{3}{2} nRT_K$$

**total kinetic energy in a
perfect gas at temperature T_K**

Note that the two "K" subscripts above refer to different features: the "kinetic" energy and the "Kelvin" temperature scale. Also, this relationship is true for any size and shape of box.

2.2.4 Reasoning with heat and temperature ideas. Note that in the previous development of ideas regarding forces, momentum, energy, pressure, and volume, we made a number of assumptions. For instance, the total kinetic energy does not include any rotational contributions, therefore, we are assuming that the gas is made up of point objects. Also, we did not mention potential energy, but concentrated on kinetic energy. This is because we assume that a perfect gas does not have any potential energy.

These assumptions can affect how we reason about perfect gases. The questions below show how you can reason using the concepts of heat, work, temperature, and energy.

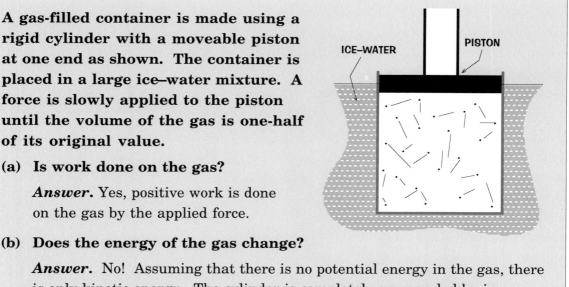

A gas-filled container is made using a rigid cylinder with a moveable piston at one end as shown. The container is placed in a large ice–water mixture. A force is slowly applied to the piston until the volume of the gas is one-half of its original value.

(a) **Is work done on the gas?**

Answer. Yes, positive work is done on the gas by the applied force.

(b) **Does the energy of the gas change?**

Answer. No! Assuming that there is no potential energy in the gas, there is only kinetic energy. The cylinder is completely surrounded by ice–water, so its temperature remains constant at 0°C. The kinetic energy only depends on temperature, so the kinetic energy remains the same.

(c) **If work is done on the gas, but the energy of the gas does not change, where does the energy go?**

Answer. Energy conservation requires that if work is done on the gas, but its energy does not change, then heat must be removed from the gas. Mathematically, $\Delta E = Q + W$. W is positive and ΔE is zero, so Q is negative, which means that heat flows <u>out</u> of the gas into the ice–water mixture.

Real gases are not perfect, but many general results remain true. Real gases are not point objects, so they spin. They are also often made up of molecules, so they have vibrational (i.e., spring-like) behavior, which means there is potential energy. Therefore, when energy is put into a system of real gases, some of the energy can go into potential energy. Solids and liquids are far from perfect gases, but in most cases, increased temperature is associated with increased motion. In the next section we begin our study of *entropy*.

2.3 ENTROPY

The term *entropy* is often defined to be the equivalent of *disorder*, but what does this mean, and what is the connection between disorder and physical systems? Can we predict whether a system will change with time or remain the same? What physical characteristics affect the entropy of a system? In this section, we will answer these questions.

2.3.1 Microstates and macrostates. To properly discuss entropy and disorder, we need to focus on the behavior of systems and how they change with time. In order to notice any changes in the system, we need to keep track of the components of a system.

There are two primary ways of labeling the states of a system. The first is by identifying the *microstates* of the system. To do this, you must be able to identify the state of every component of the system. For instance, for a system of 3 coins, there are 8 microstates: HHH, HHT, HTH, THH, HTT, THT, HTT, and TTT, where the first character refers to the side showing on the first coin, the second character refers to the second coin, etc. For N coins, there are 2^N microstates. For 2 dice, there are 36 microstates and for 3 dice there are 216 microstates. For N dice, there are 6^N microstates.

The number of microstates increases rapidly as the number of components increases. Therefore, we often use the idea of a *macrostate*, which does not keep track of the individual states, but only keeps track of the total number of components in each state. For instance, a system of 3 coins has only 4 macrostates: H^3, H^2T, HT^2, and T^3. Now, the order of the states does not matter (that is, TH^2 is the same macrostate as H^2T) and the exponent refers to the number of components in that state. (Exponents of 1 and 0 are not shown, but implied.) The table to the right shows the macrostates and the associated microstates of some different systems.

System	Macrostates	Microstates
1 coin	H	H
	T	T
2 coins	H^2	HH
	HT	HT, TH
	T^2	TT
3 coins	H^3	HHH
	H^2T	HHT, HTH, THH
	HT^2	HTT, THT, TTH
	T^3	TTT
2 dice	1^2	1 1
	1 2	1 2, 2 1
	1 3	1 3, 3 1
	1 4	1 4, 4 1
	1 5	1 5, 5 1
	1 6	1 6, 6 1
	2^2	2 2
	2 3	2 3, 3 2
	2 4	2 4, 4 2
	2 5	2 5, 5 2
	2 6	2 6, 6 2
	3^2	3 3
	3 4	3 4, 4 3
	3 5	3 5, 5 3
	3 6	3 6, 6 3
	etc.	etc.

2.3.2 Going to a large number of components. When the number of components N becomes larger than just a few, it becomes more difficult to specify the individual microstates of the system. For instance, a system of 20 coins has $(2)^{20} \approx 1$ million microstates, but only 21 macrostates. The histogram below shows the number of microstates associated with each macrostate.

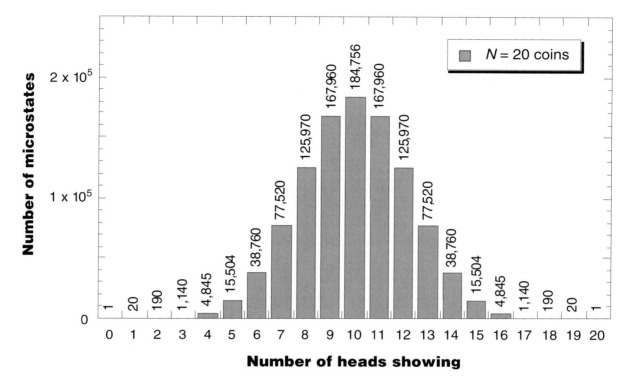

Note that each macrostate is uniquely identified by the number of heads (or tails) showing, because the total number of coins is always equal to 20. The most likely macrostate is the one in which the number of heads is equal to the number of tails.

2.3.3 Random processes and their effect on the macrostate of a system. Imagine that we start with a box of 20 coins and arrange them so that all of them show heads on the upper surface. Close the box and shake it a few times. What do you expect to see when you open the box?

It is almost 100% certain that you will <u>not</u> find all the coins still facing up! At least one or two will flip to tails up, which means that the macrostate of the system has changed. Close the box and shake it again. What happens?

Again, some coins will flip sides, but because there are so many more heads than tails, it is much more likely that one of the heads will flip than one of the tails. In other words, each coin is equally likely to flip, but there just are not very many tails in the box, so it is likely that one or two more heads will flip to tails.

As you continue to shake the box, the number of tails will continue to increase until the number of heads is approximately equal to the number of tails. After that, when you shake the box it is almost equally likely that one of the heads will flip as one of the tails, and thus, it is likely that the number of heads will stay about the same. And whenever the number of tails is not equal to the number of heads, for whichever there are more of—heads or tails—it is more likely that one of them will flip, which means that the number of heads will always fluctuate around the average value of 10. However, the size of the fluctuations may be larger than you think.

Shaking the box is an example of a random process, and 10 is the *thermodynamic* equilibrium number of heads for this system. It does <u>not</u> mean that the number of heads is always equal to 10 or even that the number of heads is close to 10, but it <u>does</u> mean that on average the number of heads is close to 10. This distinction is very important. The following graph shows the results of a computer-generated list of the number of heads for each shake assuming that there is a one-in-ten chance that any particular coin will flip during a particular shake of the box. In other words, on average, 2 of the 20 coins will flip. The graph also shows the average number of heads, where the average is done over the previous 200 shakes.

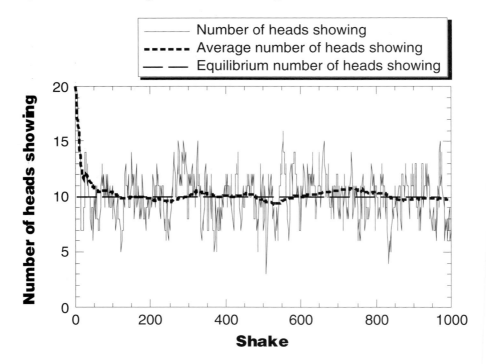

We start with 20 heads showing. After a few shakes, the number of heads is 15. After a few more, the number of heads is 10. You might think that the number of heads would then stay close to 10, but it does not. Even though the actual value of the number of heads after any particular shake ranges from 5 to 15, the average fluctuates only from about 9.3 to about 10.7.

2.3.4 Entropy and microstates. States of a physical system, such as a collection of perfect gas particles confined to a box, are often described by large-scale or macroscopic quantities such as volume, pressure, and temperature. By analogy, we are able to define the macroscopic quantity *entropy* in terms of the microstates in the system. In particular, the volume and temperature of a gas are both (separately) analogous to the number of heads facing up in a collection of two-sided coins. We are also able to relate the process of labeling and identifying states to the idea of *thermodynamic equilibrium*.

Knowing some property of a complex system may not tell us anything about the individual components of the system. For instance, if you know that a system of 4 coins is in the 4-head (H^4) state you know the state of every individual coin in the system, because there is only one way of arranging the coins (HHHH). However, if you are told that there are 2 heads and 2 tails, all you know is that the system can be in any one of 6 microstates (HHTT, HTTH, HTHT, etc.). Viewed another way, if you are told that there are 2 heads and 2 tails, you know nothing about the state of any particular coin. This is because for 3 of the 6 possible microstates, that particular coin is in the head state while for the other 3, it is in the tail state.

The "headness" of a system of 4 coins has 5 possible values: 0H, 1H, 2H, 3H, and 4H. This "headness" is analogous to a macroscopic quantity. The 2H-state (H^2T^2) has the largest number of microstates associated with it (6). A new macroscopic quantity called *entropy* is defined to be a measure of the number of states available to the components of a complex system.

ENTROPY

A measure of the number of microstates available to a system in a particular macrostate.

However, the entropy is not equal to the number of microstates. When there is only one microstate available to a system, we define the entropy to be zero. As the number of microstates increases, the entropy increases *logarithmically* as shown in the graph below. Thus, for example, the state with 1 million (10^6) microstates has twice the entropy as the state with 1,000 (10^3) microstates.

Therefore, the 4H state of a four-coin system has the <u>smallest</u> entropy (i.e., zero), because there is only one microstate associated with it, and the 2H state has the <u>largest</u> entropy, because for four coins, it is the state with the most microstates associated with it (i.e., 6).

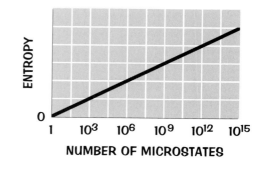

We can now characterize the *thermodynamic* equilibrium state of a complex system. (This is different from but similar to *thermal* equilibrium.)

THERMODYNAMIC EQUILIBRIUM

The thermodynamic state of maximum entropy.

Assuming all the microstates of a complex system are equally likely to occur, the thermodynamic equilibrium state is the state of maximum entropy. So, for example, in a system of 4 normal coins, the 2H state is the most likely and therefore the equilibrium state. This state has the most microstates (6) consistent with its macroscopic quantities (2H and 2T).

2.3.5 Relationship between entropy and disorder. In a system of 20 coins, the macrostates having 20 heads or 20 tails contain the most information about the individual states of the coins. In particular, there is exactly one microstate associated with each of these macrostates. These two states are said to be *highly ordered*, because these states are the *least random* states possible for the system. In other words, if you randomly pick any one of the coins, the side facing up will be the same every time. These two states also have the least entropy, because there is only one microstate associated with it. Knowing the macrostate (20H or 20T) completely determines the states of every component of the system.

As you go toward the equilibrium state of the system (i.e., 10 heads and 10 tails) the order of the system becomes less. For instance, when there are 18 heads and 2 tails, there are only 190 possible microstates. When you choose a coin at random, now there is a 90% chance of picking up a heads. This state is relatively ordered, but not as ordered as 20 heads, so its entropy is larger than the 20H state.

At the equilibrium state, there are more than 180,000 possible microstates. This state is said to be the most highly disordered, because it has the most possible microstates associated with it. We know the state is in one of the microstates, but we do not know which one. When you choose a coin at random, you have an equal chance of picking up heads or tails. It is also the state of highest entropy, so that is why we often equate *entropy* and *disorder*.

This is also a connection between entropy and information. When a system is in thermodynamic equilibrium, the values of the macroscopic quantities provide the least possible information about the actual microstate of the system. When a system has zero entropy, that means that there is only one microstate available to it, which provides the most information about the microstates of the individual components. This is why entropy is sometimes referred to as the <u>lack</u> of information about a system. The larger the entropy, the greater the lack of information about the particular microstate of any individual component of the system.

2.3.6 When the states are not equally likely. Note that if the states used to label the components of the system are not equally likely, then you must be careful when you use this definition to determine the thermodynamic equilibrium state. For instance, imagine a collection of dice for which two sides have a dot on it, but the other 4 sides are blank. There are 2 possibilities for the upper face of each die—1 or 0—but they are not equally likely to occur. There are 4 ways of getting a blank and only 2 ways of getting a dot. So, for a system of 12 dice, there are 13 macrostates, but the macrostate with 6 dots showing (and 6 blanks showing) is not the most likely state. In other words, in the previous example, when we had 20 coins, there were two equally likely possibilities for each coin, and the most likely macrostate was the one with an equal number of heads and tails. In this case, the 2 possibilities are not equally likely, so the most likely macrostate is not the one with an equal number of dots and blanks. The histogram below shows the number of microstates associated with each macrostate.

(ALL OTHER SIDES ARE BLANK)

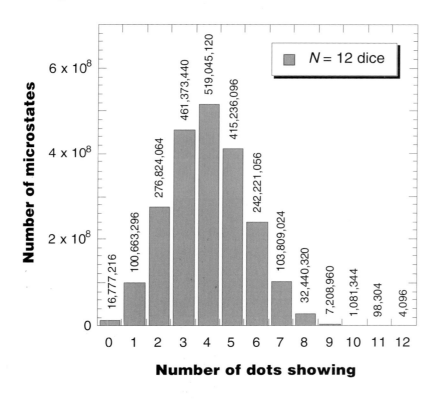

The most likely macrostate is when 4 dots are showing, therefore this is the state of maximum entropy. This is also the equilibrium state of the system. This makes sense, because there is a one-in-three chance that a dot will be showing, so out of 12 dice, we expect 4 of them to be showing a dot. Note that the distribution is skewed toward the more likely states, in this case, the states with more blanks. This means that at the two extremes—no dots and 12 dots showing—there are different numbers of microstates, which means that the entropies of the two extreme states are not the same. In this system, the state with 12 dots showing is the state having the smallest entropy. Further, the states with 9, 10, and 11 dots showing each has an entropy that is smaller than the state with no dots showing, because each of them is less likely to occur.

2.3.7 Applying entropy ideas to perfect gases. Although the ideas surrounding entropy were developed using relatively small complex systems, they are particularly useful for analyzing much larger systems, such as a collection of 10^{23} perfect gas particles. The analysis remains largely the same: Label the microstates and macrostates of the system. Determine the macrostate with the most number of microstates associated with it. This is the state with the highest entropy, so it is the thermodynamic equilibrium state as well.

The microstates of a gas consist of the labeling of the position and velocity of each gas particle in the system. The macrostates depend on the volume and temperature of the system. In other words, there is a close relationship between the positions available to a particular gas particle and the volume of the container—the larger the volume, the larger the number of possible positions. There is also a close relationship between the velocities available to a gas particle and the temperature of the gas—the larger the temperature, the larger the number of possible sets of velocities. This relationship is represented graphically in the diagram below.

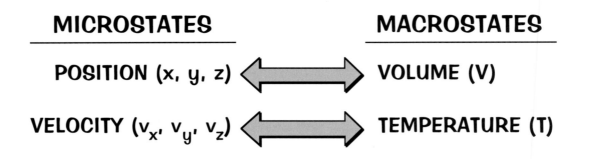

MICROSTATES		MACROSTATES
POSITION (x, y, z)	⟺	VOLUME (V)
VELOCITY (v_x, v_y, v_z)	⟺	TEMPERATURE (T)

Entropy also depends on the number of gas particles, because your knowledge of the state of any individual particle depends on the number of particles. For instance, going back to the examples involving coins, the equilibrium state of 4 coins has 6 microstates associated with it. The equilibrium state of 20 coins has more than 180,000 microstates associated with it. Therefore, the entropy is different for the two macrostates, even though they are both at equilibrium. The system with more components generally has more entropy, but not always. You must first look at the number of microstates available, then decide which has more entropy.

2.3.8 Reasoning with entropy ideas. In the following examples, we show a few of the contexts in which entropy ideas may be successfully applied. Keep in mind that coins and perfect gases are not the only systems we can study, but any system that undergoes changes.

In this first example, there are two different types of coins, which affects the results dramatically.

Eight 2-headed coins and 12 normal coins are placed in a box. There is a one-in-five chance that one of the coins will flip sides during any particular shake of the box.

(a) What is the equilibrium state of the system?

Answer. Assuming that the two sides of the 2-headed coins are the same, then the equilibrium state is 14 heads facing up, because all (8) of the 2-headed coins and half of the normal coins (6) would be heads up.

(b) List all the states that have the least entropy.

Answer. There are two: the state with 20 heads showing, and the state with 8 heads and 12 tails showing. For each, there are exactly $2^8 = 256$ microstates associated with it. In each of these states, there is only one way to arrange the normal coins: all heads or all tails. But there are 256 ways to arrange the 2-headed coins, even though 8 heads are always showing.

(c) How would the answers above change if the probability of flipping was one-in-ten instead?

Answer. The answers would not change. The equilibrium state and the states of least entropy are identified by counting microstates. The process by which equilibrium is achieved does not matter.

(d) How would the answers change if the probability of getting a heads was twice as likely as getting a tails?

Answer. The answers would change. The probability of getting a heads is $2/3$ and the probability of getting a tails is $1/3$. The equilibrium state is now 16 heads facing up, with all of the 2-headed coins and two-thirds of the "normal" coins facing heads up. The macrostate with the least number of microstates is the one with 8 heads and 12 tails, so this is the state with the least entropy.

In this next example, we apply entropy ideas to a perfect gas.

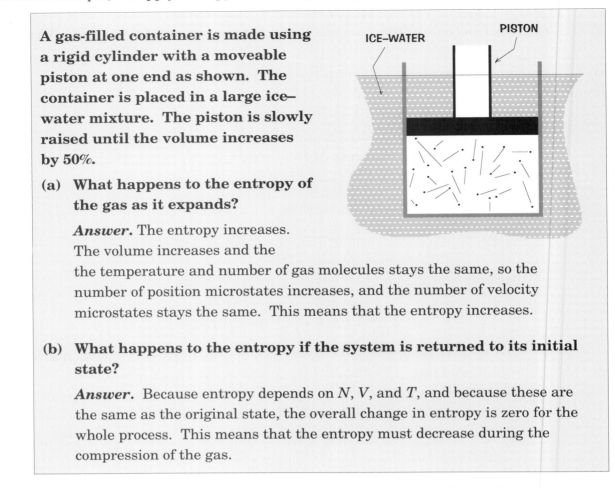

A gas-filled container is made using a rigid cylinder with a moveable piston at one end as shown. The container is placed in a large ice–water mixture. The piston is slowly raised until the volume increases by 50%.

(a) **What happens to the entropy of the gas as it expands?**

Answer. The entropy increases. The volume increases and the the temperature and number of gas molecules stays the same, so the number of position microstates increases, and the number of velocity microstates stays the same. This means that the entropy increases.

(b) **What happens to the entropy if the system is returned to its initial state?**

Answer. Because entropy depends on N, V, and T, and because these are the same as the original state, the overall change in entropy is zero for the whole process. This means that the entropy must decrease during the compression of the gas.

Whenever a perfect gas returns to the same macrostate—i.e., same N, V, and T—the entropy of the gas also returns to the same value. It does not matter what has happened to the gas in between.

Note that if the gas is not kept at constant temperature, having the gas do work (by having it push on the piston) will lower its temperature and therefore decrease the number of velocity microstates available to the gas particles. Since the volume is increasing—which increases the entropy—and the temperature is decreasing—which decreases the entropy—we do not have enough information to determine how the entropy is changing.

Through the Perfect Gas Law, we can also use pressure to represent changes in a gas.

A certain amount of gas is taken around the cycle shown below. The first process is at constant temperature as the gas is taken from point 1 to point 2. The second process is at constant pressure, ending at point 3, and the third is at constant volume, taking the gas back to point 1 again.

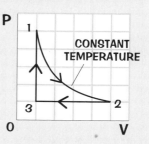

(a)   Describe how each of the processes might be made to occur.

Answer. Imagine that the gas is in a container with a piston, as in the previous example, and start at point 1. The constant temperature process can be made to occur by immersing the container in a large amount of water or other material at that particular temperature and using the piston to slowly let the gas expand until it reaches point 2. The constant pressure process can be achieved by keeping the force constant and lowering the temperature of the gas until reaching point 3. The constant volume process can be done by holding the piston in a fixed position and increasing the temperature until returning to point 1 again.

(b)   At which point does the gas have the largest entropy?

Answer. At point 2. Because entropy depends on V and T, it is a little easier to see why by going to a V vs. T plot of the same cycle.

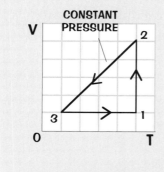

Going from point 1 to point 2 is a constant temperature process, as shown, which is a vertical line in this plot for which the volume increases. Going from point 2 to point 3 is a constant pressure process, which is a diagonal line. Going from 3 back to 1 is a constant volume process during which the temperature rises. Since point 2 has the highest temperature and the largest volume, it has the most velocity states and the most position states associated with it, so it also has the highest entropy.

For a perfect gas, $PV \sim NT$. When N and T are constant, as in going from point 1 to point 2 above, $P \sim 1/V$, which means that P vs. V is curved. When N and P are constant, as in going from point 2 to point 3 above, $V \sim T$, which means that V vs. T is a sloped line.

This concludes the chapter on *heat*, *temperature*, and *entropy*.

COMPLEX SYSTEMS
READER
CHAPTER 3

OSCILLATIONS AND WAVES

According to the atomic model, all matter consists of huge numbers of interacting particles in the form of atoms. Because atoms interact, a disturbance in one region of a material will spread to other regions as time passes. So, for example, when a pebble is dropped into a puddle of water, the pebble exerts forces on the water particles with which it comes in contact. In response to these forces, the water particles momentarily move away from their equilibrium position. As a result, they exert forces on other nearby water particles, causing them to temporarily move away from equilibrium. The whole process continues so that the disturbance of the water, which was initially confined to the region near where the pebble entered the puddle, spreads out over time across the entire puddle. Even though the disturbance has moved to other parts of the puddle, the particles of water move back (more or less) to their original equilibrium positions. Phenomena like this in which a disturbance moves through a medium is called a *wave*. The repetitive nature of the motion of the water molecules as they move back and forth near their equilibrium positions is called *oscillations*.

There are two sections in this chapter, one each dealing with oscillations and waves. In the first, you will learn how to apply force and energy ideas to oscillating systems. You will also learn some new concepts such as *frequency*, *amplitude*, and *period*, and how they apply to oscillators. In the second section you will learn about wave phenomena. You will again apply force and energy ideas to waves, then you will learn about *standing waves*, *traveling waves*, the *interference* of waves, and the *transmission* and *reflection* of waves at an interface between two media.

3.1 OSCILLATIONS

Why do some oscillating objects move back and forth more quickly than others? In other words, why do some systems take less time to return to their original configurations than others? What factors affect the behavior of oscillating systems? What happens when there are two or more objects moving at the same time? These and other questions will be answered in this section, primarily by analyzing oscillating systems using force and energy ideas.

3.1.1 Analyzing oscillations using forces. It is useful to locate and focus on the equilibrium position or balance point of the oscillator—the position at which the net force on the oscillator is zero when it is at rest. For a mass hanging from a spring, this is where the spring is stretched an amount $d = mg/k$, because there the spring force (kd, up) balances the gravitational force (mg, down). For a bob on a string, this is where the angle relative to the vertical is zero. Note that the balance point is labeled with the subscript eq to indicate that it is the equilibrium position.

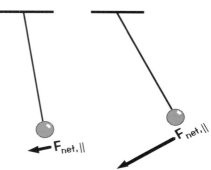

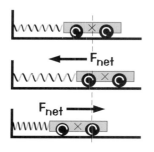

The component of the net force on an oscillator along the direction of motion often points back toward the balance point. So, for example, for a cart attached to a spring, the net force is to the left when the cart is moved to the right, and to the right when it is moved to the left. Note that the direction of the force does <u>not</u> depend on the direction of motion.

The component of the net force along the direction of motion may increase as the oscillator is pulled or pushed farther from the balance point. So, for a bob on a string, the farther the string is moved from the vertical, the larger the net force parallel to the motion of the bob.

For many oscillating systems, the force law is linear (e.g., the spring force kd), which results in sinusoidal motion, i.e., $y(t) = y_{eq} + A\cos(2\pi ft)$, where y_{eq} is the oscillator's balance point, A is the *amplitude* of the motion, f is the frequency of oscillation, and we have assumed that the oscillator is initially at rest. The sequence of diagrams below shows the position of a mass as it oscillates up and down on a spring. The diagrams are equally spaced in time, so the horizontal axis may be considered the time axis. The dotted line shows the plot of y vs. t, and the dashed line indicates the balance point.

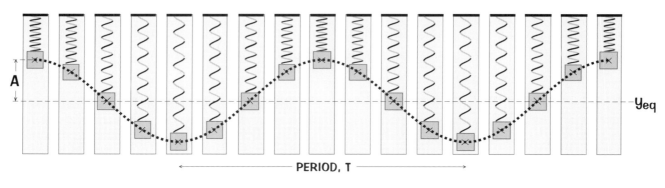

Note that the position of the oscillator is always between $y = y_{eq} + A$ and $y = y_{eq} - A$. Also, sometimes it is more convenient to analyze the motion of an oscillator in terms of the *period T*, which is the time between repetitions. Because the frequency f is the number of repetitions per second, $T = 1/f$. In other words, the period T is the number of seconds per repetition.

For a mass on a spring, the frequency of oscillation f depends on only two factors: the mass m and the spring constant k. When the mass is large, it is harder to accelerate the mass, so the time it takes to complete each cycle gets large, and the frequency gets small. When the spring constant is large, the force at each point in the motion is larger, so the acceleration is larger, the time it takes to complete each cycle gets smaller, and the frequency gets larger. Mathematically:

$$f = \frac{1}{2\pi}\sqrt{\frac{k}{m}}$$

frequency of oscillation for a mass on a spring

We can also determine the frequency of oscillation for a bob swinging on a string. We measure the distance s along the path of the bob, as shown on the far left below. (Note that the balance point is $s = 0$.)

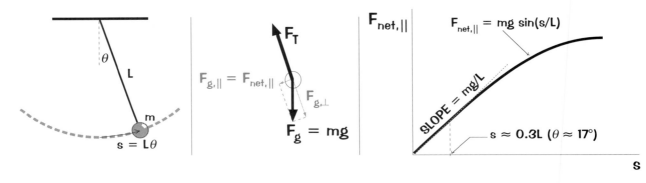

There are only two forces on the bob: the tension force exerted by the string, and a gravitational force exerted by the Earth, as shown in the middle above. Only the gravitational force has a component along the path of the bob, so the force law governing the motion of the bob is $F_{net,\parallel} = F_{g,\parallel} = mg\sin\theta = mg\sin(s/L)$, where L is the length of the string. This force law is not linear except at small distances from the bottom of the path. A plot of the force $F_{net,\parallel}$ vs. s is shown on the far right above. Just as the slope of force vs. position for a mass on a spring is k, the effective spring constant for small angles is mg/L. Mathematically:

$$f = \frac{1}{2\pi}\sqrt{\frac{g}{L}}$$

frequency of oscillation for a bob on a string

Therefore, the frequency of oscillation has the remarkable feature of being independent of the mass of the bob when the amplitude of oscillation is relatively small ($\theta_{max} < 17°$). Also, the longer the string, the smaller the frequency, and the longer it takes to complete each cycle.

3.1.2 Analyzing oscillations using energy ideas. You may need to review the expressions for kinetic and potential energy. For instance, a rigid, non-rotating object has kinetic energy $\frac{1}{2}mv^2$. The gravitational potential energy in any Earth–mass system is mgy, where y is the height of the mass above a well defined reference height. The elastic (or spring) potential energy is $\frac{1}{2}kd^2$, where d is how far the ideal spring is compressed or stretched from its relaxed state. Note that for a mass hanging from a vertical spring, the relaxed state is not the same as the equilibrium state.

If no macroscopic energy becomes microscopic energy and if there are no interactions with other objects or systems, then changes in the kinetic energy—e.g., $\Delta(\frac{1}{2}mv^2)$—must be compensated by changes in potential energy—e.g., $\Delta(mgy + \frac{1}{2}kd^2)$. This means that when the kinetic energy is a maximum, the potential energy is a minimum, and vice versa.

Reconsider the situation in which a cart is attached to a spring, which is attached to a wall. The spring has an elastic constant k, the cart has mass m, and the position x is measured from the wall as shown.

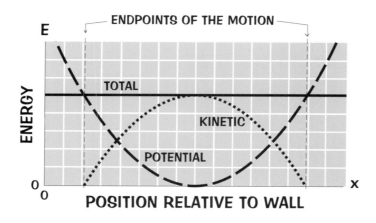

Plots of energy vs. position x are shown to the left. The total, kinetic, and potential energies are shown as a solid, dotted, and dashed line, respectively. Note that the total energy is the same at every position x. The height y is constant, so if we define the height to be zero, the potential energy is due to the spring only. Where the potential energy is smallest is where the net force on the cart is zero, which is the equilibrium or balance point of the motion. Near the endpoints of the motion, the kinetic energy becomes very small and the potential energy becomes close to its maximum value for this particular total energy. Note that the potential energy curve gets even larger when the cart is farther from its equilibrium position, but the motion stops when the potential energy is equal to the total energy, because there the kinetic energy is zero.

Plots of energy vs. time are also informative. Assuming that the cart is displaced and released from rest, the total, kinetic, and potential energies vs. time are shown at the top of the next page. The total energy, as indicated by the solid, horizontal line is the same at every instant. The initial kinetic energy is zero, because the cart is initially at rest. Therefore, all of the energy in the situation is in the elastic potential energy of the spring. After the cart is released, it speeds up, so the kinetic energy gets larger. Meanwhile, the spring is returning to its relaxed length, so the potential energy is getting smaller. When the spring reaches its relaxed length, the potential energy is zero, and the cart's kinetic energy is maximum and equal to the total energy. At all times the sum of the kinetic and potential energies is the total energy.

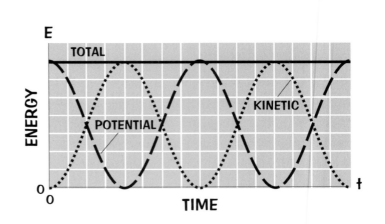

Note that we cannot tell from this second set of plots whether the cart is displaced to the left or to the right before it is released. In either case, the initial kinetic energy is zero and the initial potential energy is maximum and equal to the total energy.

3.1.3 Reasoning about oscillations.

Consider the following plot of potential energy vs. position, where the energy is given in Joules (J) and the position is given in meters (m). Assuming that the total energy E is 3J, what would a sketch of position vs. time look like?

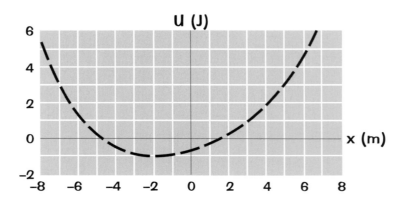

First we should determine the endpoints of the motion. Assuming that there are no dissipative effects, such as friction or air resistance, the total energy is constant at 3J. This means it is the same at every position, as shown by the solid, horizontal line below.

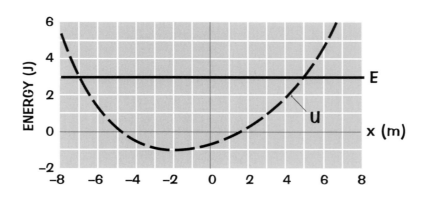

The kinetic energy is the difference between E and U, that is, $E_K = E - U$. This means that when $E = U$, the kinetic energy is zero, and the object stops. According to the plot, this occurs at $x = -7$m and $x = 5$m. Therefore, the object oscillates between these two extremes.

Next, let's find out where the speed of the object is largest. The balance point is where the potential energy is a minimum (like the bottom of a bowl). This occurs at $x = -2$m. This is also where the kinetic energy of the object is largest, so its speed is largest there as well. The solid curve below shows the position of the object as a function of time assuming that the object is released from rest at $x = -7$m.

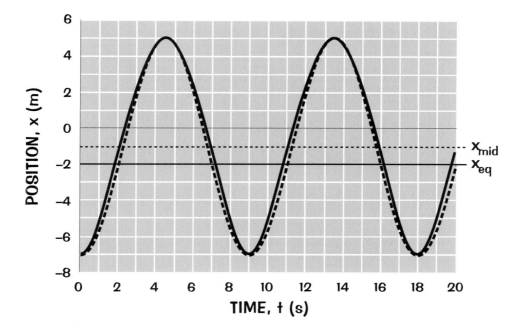

The slope of the solid curve is largest at around $t = 1.8$s, because this is when it reaches the equilibrium position. (Remember that the slope of position vs. time is velocity vs. time.) It then takes about another 2.7s to reach the other limit ($x = 5$m) before turning around and going back again. Each cycle takes about 9 seconds to complete. Although the solid curve is periodic, it is not sinusoidal. For comparison, a cosine function with the same limits and frequency is shown as a dotted line. It oscillates around the midpoint $x_{mid} = 1$m and is noticeably different than the solid curve.

The mass takes less time to reach the equilibrium position from the left because the slope of the potential energy vs. position is larger there. During each cycle, the mass spends about 40% of the time on the left-hand side of x_{eq} and the other 60% on the right-hand side of x_{eq}.

We can understand this difference in the times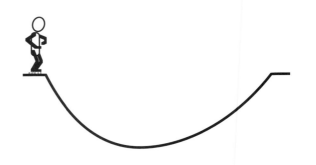
using an analogy. Imagine a roller blading course
in which the curved walls are the same shape as
the potential curve. The potential energy is *mgy*,
so $U(x)$ has the same functional form (i.e., the
same shape) in both cases. If you roll a marble
from the left-hand side, it will take less time to
reach the bottom than it will to reach the top of
the other side, because the wall is steeper on the left than on the right. (The motion of the
roller blader is more complicated because there is non-negligible friction and because he can
put in or take out energy using his legs and body.)

3.1.4 Oscillations in complex systems. Oscillatory motion is not limited to single objects.
For instance, if two or three objects are connected by springs, then the resulting motion is
more elaborate, but it is often still oscillatory. Consider the following situation involving three
springs and two masses. The middle spring has an elastic constant that is 50% larger than
each of the other two, and the system is released from rest as shown on the right.

Immediately after the masses are released, there is a net force on the mass *A* to the left which
causes it to start moving to the left, and a net force on mass *B* to the right which causes it to
move to the right. Graphs of the positions of the two masses are shown below.

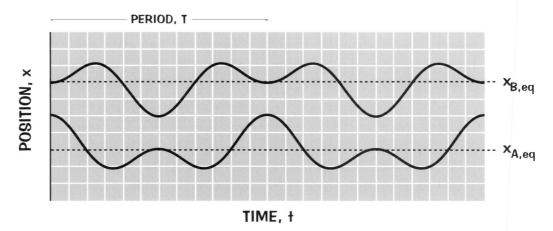

The motion is complicated but periodic: when the masses return to their original positions and
velocities, the motion repeats itself. The time it takes to complete one cycle is the period *T*
indicated in the diagram.

It is informative to look at how energy is distributed through the system and how it changes with time. There are five objects to consider: each of the three springs has a potential energy, and each mass has a kinetic energy. Assuming that the springs are relaxed when the masses are in equilibrium, the potential energies are $\frac{1}{2}k_1(x_A - x_{A,eq})^2$ for the left-hand spring, $\frac{1}{2}k_3(x_B - x_{B,eq})^2$ for the right-hand spring, and $\frac{1}{2}k_2(x_A - x_B - x_{A,eq} + x_{B,eq})^2$ for the middle spring. The kinetic energies are $\frac{1}{2}mv_A^2$ and $\frac{1}{2}mv_B^2$ for the two masses. Graphs of the energy vs. time are shown below.

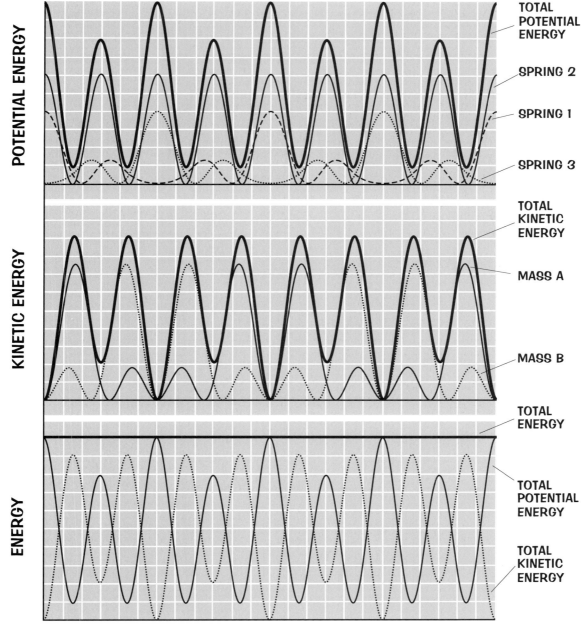

At the top are plots of potential energy vs. time. Initially, the distance that spring #2 is compressed is the same as the distance that spring #1 is stretched. But spring #2 is 50% stiffer than spring #1, so its initial potential energy is 50% larger than that of spring #1. Spring #3 is relaxed initially, so its initial potential energy is zero. As time evolves, the lengths of the springs change, which results in the total potential energy shown as a solid line. Note that there are exactly two complete cycles shown here, just as there were in the plots of position vs. time on the previous page.

The middle set of plots shows the kinetic energies as functions of time. All are initially zero, because both masses are at rest initially. By looking at the plot for either mass A or mass B, you can see that the curves repeat only once, not three times. For instance, the plot for mass A begins with a large bump, followed by two small bumps, followed by another large bump. This pattern repeats once more in the time period shown.

In spite of the complicated pattern, the total kinetic energy and total potential energy sum to a constant at all times, as shown on the bottom set of curves. The total energy is a solid, horizontal line, indicating that it does not change as time evolves.

3.1.5 Periodic vs. non-periodic motion. The previous situation is an example of *periodic* oscillatory motion because the resulting behavior of the two masses has a definite time period over which it repeats. It happens in this case because of the particular ratios chosen for the spring constants and masses.

Non-periodic oscillatory motion is more common. It is what usually occurs in nature when there are interacting objects oscillating back and forth. It is recognized by the absence of a pattern or the absence of a definite time period over which the motion of the components of the complex system repeats. For instance, if we choose k_2 to be three times as stiff as k_1, and use the same initial situation, the following plots of position vs. time result.

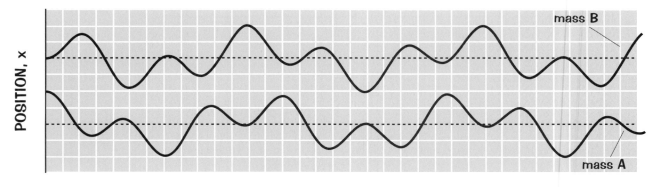

TIME, t

Now, even though a longer time interval is shown, there appears to be no well defined period, because the motion does not repeat .

3.1.6 Normal modes. The previous situation is also excellent for introducing and understanding the concept of *normal modes*. A normal mode is periodic behavior in which <u>every</u> component of the system oscillates back and forth with the <u>same</u> frequency. For many systems, periodic behavior is possible only when the system is in a normal mode.

An example will help. The situation is shown to the right. Assume that the masses are identical, and that the middle spring is different from the other two.

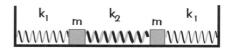

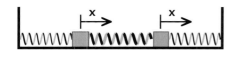

The first normal mode occurs when both masses move the same amount and in the same direction as shown. The middle spring never changes its length, so the force on each mass is $k_1 x$. Therefore both masses oscillate back and forth with the same frequency of $1/2\pi \sqrt{k_1/m}$.

The second normal mode occurs when both masses move the same amount but in opposite directions. The force on each mass is $(k_1 + 2k_2)x$, so both masses oscillate with the same frequency of $1/2\pi \sqrt{(k_1 + 2k_2)/m}$. Note that the masses always oscillate faster in this mode, because $(2k_2 + k_1)$ is always larger than k_1.

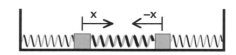

We can now redraw the graphs of position vs. time for the two masses, this time showing the contributions from the two normal modes. (The particular graphs for the normal modes are determined by the initial situation.) In this case, $k_2 = 3k_1$, so the second normal mode has a frequency that is $\sqrt{7}$ times as large as that of the first. This means that the period of the second normal mode is $1/\sqrt{7}$ as large as that of the first.

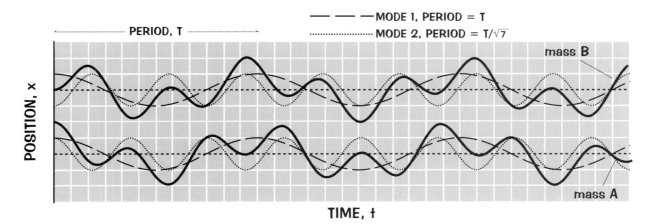

There are three important features of this graph that you should notice: (1) In mode 1, the two masses move the same distance, in the same direction, and with the same frequency. This frequency is smaller than in mode 2. (2) In mode 2, the two masses move the same distance, in opposite directions, and with the same frequency. This frequency is larger than in mode 1. (3) The sum of the two curves at every instant is equal to the resulting solid curves, which represent the actual behavior of the two masses.

In this section, we have shown you how to recognize, analyze, and understand oscillatory motion for one and two particle systems. The ideas developed here can also be applied to systems with any number of components, all the way up to *continuous complex systems*. Such systems include water waves, a humming tuning fork, and a vibrating guitar string, which can be thought of as an infinite number of infinitely small interacting objects.

In the next section, we begin the study of waves. Most often, we will look for additional examples of periodic behavior, such as the normal modes found for two masses and three springs. We will again apply force and energy ideas, and we will look for patterns and principles that we can use to discuss, explain, and understand wave phenomena.

3.2 WAVES

Waves occur throughout nature and are at the heart of many important physical phenomena such as earthquakes, music, ultrasound, and light. A simple model you may find useful for thinking about waves is a system of objects connected by springs. The objects play the role of atoms, while the springs model the interactions between atoms. If we shake a few of the objects, they will move away from equilibrium. As these objects move about, their attached springs will change length and orientation, leading to a net force on neighboring objects, which in turn will lead to motion of their neighboring objects, leading to forces on objects still further away. The objects do not move far from their original positions because the springs exert forces that tend to restore them to equilibrium. Even though this model is too simplistic to describe adequately the behavior of realistic materials, it does depict many of the essential features that lead to waves.

3.2.1 Analyzing waves using forces. The simplest disturbance to analyze is a vibrating string. Consider the following situation in which a string is vibrating as shown in the strobe diagram below.

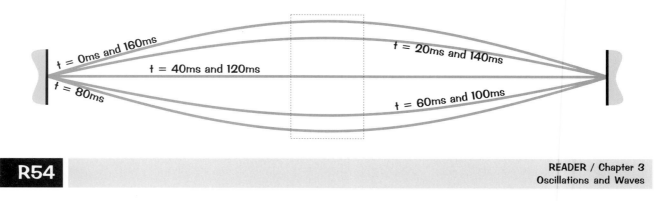

The motion of the string repeats itself every 160 milliseconds (1 millisecond = 0.001s = 1ms). Looking at the boxed segment at $t = 0$ms, we find that the net force is not zero, because the string is curved. The tension forces on the string balance in the horizontal direction but add in the vertical direction for a net force downward. (We assume that the gravitational force on this piece of string is negligible, so it is missing from the diagram below.) At the extremes of the motion ($t = 0$ms, 80ms, and 160ms), the speed of the string is zero. The string speeds up as it approaches its equilibrium position because the net force is in the direction of motion.

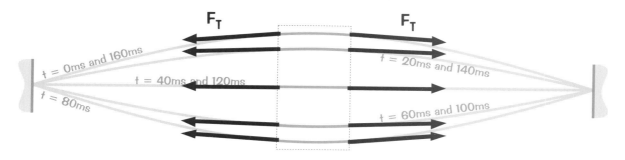

Plots of position, velocity, and acceleration vs. time are shown below for the middle of the string. At $t = 40$ms, when the string is horizontal ($y = 0$), the net force on the piece of string is zero, so a_y is zero, but the string is moving downward. This is also when the string is moving the fastest. As the string continues downward, the net force is now upward, while the velocity is downward, which means that the string slows down. The string stops at $t = 80$ms, where the net force exerted on it is maximum again.

Because the net force is maximum when the string is farthest from equilibrium (i.e., farthest from the straight string), this is also when the acceleration is maximum.

Note that at every instant of time, the slope of the height vs. time curve is the velocity vs. time curve, and the slope of velocity vs. time is acceleration vs. time. So, for instance, at $t = 0$ms, the slope of height vs. time is zero and becoming more negative, which is exactly what is happening to the velocity vs. time curve. And between $t = 80$ms and $t = 120$ms, the slope of velocity vs. time is positive and getting smaller, just like the acceleration vs. time curve.

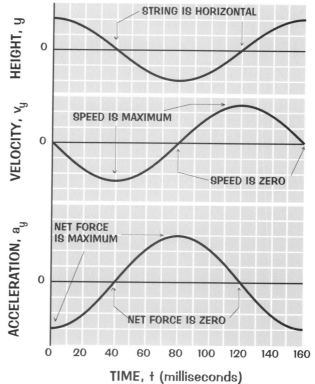

Another type of disturbance consists of a wave moving through a medium. For instance, in the situation shown below, if the left-most ball is moved to the left and released, a wave will move to the right through the system.

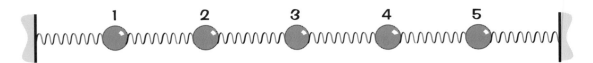

We can understand this phenomenon using forces, because initially the left two balls are not in equilibrium and therefore are accelerated. When ball 2 moves in response to the net force on it, ball 3 is no longer in equilibrium, so it moves in response to the net force on it, and so on through the system. The sequence of diagrams on the next page shows the positions of the five balls at equal time intervals after the leftmost ball is released.

The vertical, dashed lines indicate the equilibrium positions of the five balls. At instant *B*, ball 1 has moved far from its original position, but ball 2 has moved only about half as far, because it is being pulled in two different directions by the two springs attached to it, while ball 1 is being pushed/pulled to the right by both springs attached to it. Balls 3, 4, and 5 are still approximately where they started. In other words, the disturbance has not reached them yet.

At instant *C*, ball 1 has moved to the right as far as it ever does and it starts to move back toward its equilibrium position. Meanwhile, the disturbance is starting to affect balls 3 and 4 more noticeably. By instant *H*, ball 5 is experiencing the full effect of the disturbance and the wave appears to be traveling back to the left again. Note that each ball is pulled slightly to the left before being displaced to the right. This is because the net force on each ball is initially to the left, which causes it to accelerate to the left. Eventually, the net force is to the right, which causes each ball to reverse direction and reach its largest displacement to the right of its equilibrium position.

TIME

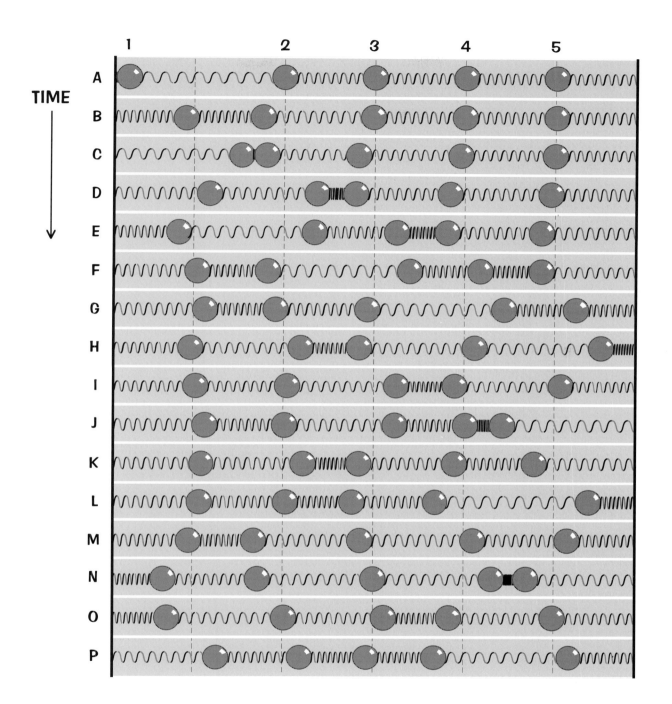

3.2.2 Analyzing waves using momentum and energy ideas. To apply momentum and energy ideas, it is useful to focus on small pieces of the medium and watch what each piece does as time evolves. This technique will help you avoid many common sources of confusion.

We start as before with a string vibrating up and down. In this case, we will concentrate on two segments of the string—one in the middle and the other at the end, as indicated by the boxes. At $t = 0$ms, 80ms, and 160ms, the string is at rest. At $t = 40$ms and 120ms, the string is horizontal.

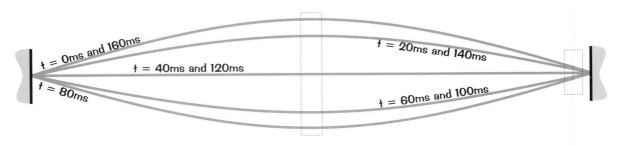

Some comments about the mass are needed before analyzing the motion of this vibrating string. Even though the segment on the right is slightly longer than the segment in the middle, both have the same mass, because it is assumed that each point along the string moves only up and down. In other words, when the string is horizontal, both pieces have the same length and therefore also the same mass. As the string vibrates, different parts stretch different amounts to give the string the shape shown. In particular, the segment on the right stretches more than the segment in the middle.

Let's start with momentum ideas. The direction of motion of each segment is always up or down, so the momentum of each is also up or down as well. Both segments have the same mass, so the speed of each will determine which has the larger momentum at any particular time. When the string is at rest, each segment is at rest, so each has zero momentum. When the string is horizontal, the middle segment is moving quickly, but the end piece is hardly moving at all, so the middle segment has the larger speed and therefore also the larger momentum.

Let's now turn to energy ideas. There are two types of energy to consider: kinetic energy and elastic potential energy. (We are ignoring the gravitational potential energy.) The kinetic energy depends on the speed of each segment. Therefore, like momentum, the kinetic energy is zero for both segments at $t = 0$ms, 80ms, and 160ms, and it is larger for the middle segment at all other times.

The elastic potential energy depends on how far each piece is stretched from its relaxed length. The string is under tension, so there is some potential energy in the system even when the string is horizontal. However, this is the smallest amount of potential energy in the string.

As the string vibrates, it stretches even more, and the potential energy increases. But the string stretches unevenly. Different parts of the string stretch more than others. In particular, the middle of the string does not stretch very much during the motion. It is approximately the same length at all times. But the end of the string stretches the most, which means that the concentration of potential energy is highest there. Thus, as the string vibrates, the potential energy in the middle of the string does not change very much, but the potential energy in the end of the string changes the most.

Looking at both the kinetic and potential energies at the same time, we find that the middle segment has minimal potential and zero kinetic energy initially, but nearly constant potential and changing kinetic energy when the string is moving. For the end segment, there is zero kinetic and maximal potential energy initially, but changing potential and almost zero kinetic energy when the string is moving. This means that energy is flowing from the ends of the string to the middle and back again during the motion of the string. The graph to the right

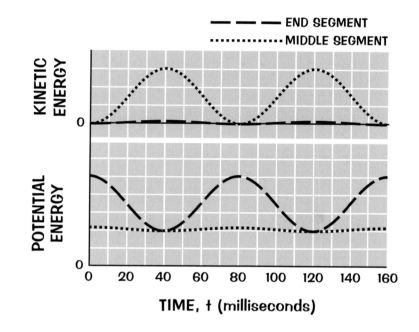

shows the kinetic and potential energies of both segments as functions of time.

Another situation is shown below. In this sequence of drawings, a disturbance is seen to travel along a spring from left to right. There are nine labeled segments. As with the vibrating string, each segment of spring has the same mass as every other one, because the spring stretches to give the observed shape.

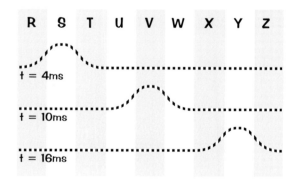

To analyze this situation, it is useful first to imagine what the spring looks like at instants in between the instants shown. The diagram on the next page shows the same situation every second between t = 4ms and t = 10ms.

Even though the wave is traveling to the right, the momentum in this situation is up and down. For instance, in segment R at t = 4ms, the rightmost coils of the spring are moving downward. (We know this, for example, because in the next instant, the segment is perfectly horizontal.) In segment U at t = 6ms, the leftmost coils of the spring are moving upward. (In the next instant the segment has moved upward.)

Energy flows from one end of the spring to the other as time evolves. Wherever the spring is stretched or moving, there is energy. So initially, there is both kinetic and potential energy in segments R and T (and a little of both in segment S). At t = 6ms, the energy has moved to segments STU, at t = 8ms, it is in TUV, and at t = 10ms, it is in UVW. Note that energy is not a vector, so it

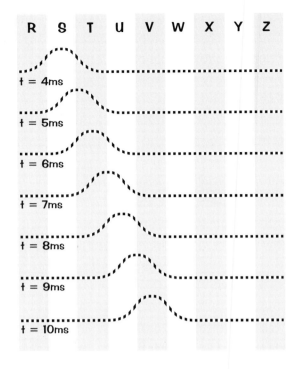

does not have a direction. Therefore, we do not say that energy is "moving" to the right, but rather that it "flows" or "is transferred" from one place to another.

3.2.3 Traveling vs. standing waves.
In the two previous sections, you have examined three situations. They have been different in a number of ways. One of the differences is that with the vibrating string the wave form did not move left or right but merely became smaller and larger as time passed. With the five masses connected to springs and with the stretched spring, the wave form moved along the medium, in these cases, left and / or right.

The vibrating string is an example of a *standing wave*. It is characterized by *nodes*, which are points of zero displacement, *wavelength*, which is the distance within the medium that the wave form repeats, and *frequency*, which is the rate at which the wave form is changing. The shapes of the lowest three frequencies of standing waves are shown in the diagram below.

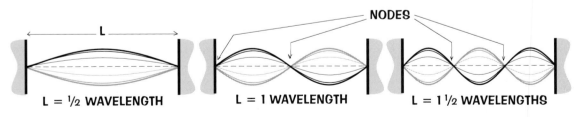

The other two situations are examples of *traveling waves*, which are characterized primarily by their speed. Both types of waves are also characterized by their *amplitudes*, which is the maximum amount that the medium is displaced from its equilibrium position. Some traveling waves have *width*, which is the amount of the medium disturbed as the wave passes.

3.2.4 Reasoning about waves. Now that we have a variety of concepts related to waves and wave phenomena, we can make and explain certain comparisons. For instance, consider a vibrating string. The string has length L, the tension in the string is F_T, and the total mass of the string is M. In the shape shown on the far left of the previous diagram, it oscillates at a certain frequency f. When we change F_T, M, or the number of nodes, what happens to f?

For a fixed total mass M and length L, changing the tension changes the acceleration of each segment of the string. The larger the tension, the larger the acceleration, and the larger the frequency of oscillation.

For a fixed length of string, changing the total mass changes the amount of mass in each segment of string. For an unchanged net force on each segment, this means that the acceleration is changed. In particular, the larger the mass of the string, the smaller the acceleration, and the smaller the frequency of oscillation.

When there are more than 2 nodes in a standing wave (there must be at least 2, i.e., the ends), the frequency is also affected. For 3 nodes (see diagram on the previous page), the string is more curved, which means that the net force on each segment is larger, <u>even though the tension has not changed</u>. This means that each segment accelerates faster than when there are only 2 nodes, which means that the frequency is larger. This pattern continues as the number of nodes increases: all else staying the same, the more nodes there are, the higher the frequency.

Consider a guitar or violin string under tension. We can change the length of the part that vibrates by pressing down on part of the string with a finger. This changes the placement of one of the nodes without changing the tension F_T or the mass per unit length M/L. In other words, both the mass and the length of the string vibrating are different, but their ratio is the same. How does the frequency of a standing wave change?

From experience, you might already know the answer, but let's see if we can explain it. The argument is similar to the one used to explain why the frequency increases with the number of nodes. Comparing two waves with the same amplitude, the wave with the smaller L has more curvature. Focusing on a segment of the string in the middle, this means that the net force is larger, so the acceleration is larger, which means that the frequency is larger as well.

A useful technique for analyzing standing waves is *dimensional analysis*. There are only four relevant quantities: total mass M, length L, tension F_T, and amplitude. We know from experience that the amplitude does not affect the frequency. For instance, when you pluck a guitar string, a larger amplitude results in a louder note, but the frequency of the note—the sensation of pitch—remains approximately the same. That leaves three quantities.

We are looking for a combination of them that has units of $1/s$ (the units of frequency), and it might appear that with only kg, m, and N to work with, no combination would work. But $1N = 1kg \cdot m/s^2$, so F_T/ML has units of $1/s^2$, and $\sqrt{F_T/ML}$ has units of $1/s$. This means that the frequency of oscillation of a guitar string is proportional to $\sqrt{F_T/ML}$, though we usually write it as $1/L\sqrt{F_T/\mu}$ where $\mu \equiv M/L$ is the mass per unit length of the string. Note that this relationship for frequency confirms all of the results deduced previously—that the frequency is larger when the tension is made larger, or when the mass is decreased, or when the length is made smaller. Also, this relationship says only that the frequency is <u>proportional</u> to $\sqrt{F_T/ML}$, not that it is equal to it.

For traveling waves, the focal concept is speed, and it depends on two quantities, tension F_T and mass per unit length $\mu = M/L$. (The speed does not depend on the mass and the length separately, because the wave form is localized within a limited region of the medium and therefore is not affected by its total length or mass.) The larger the tension, the larger the acceleration of individual segments of the medium, so the faster they return to their equilibrium positions. This means that the speed is larger when the tension is larger. The larger the mass per unit length, the smaller the acceleration, so the slower each segment returns to its equilibrium position. This means that the speed is larger when the mass per unit length is smaller.

Taken together, these two results suggest that the speed is proportional to F_T/μ. Unfortunately, a dimensional analysis of this ratio finds that it does not have the correct units:

$$\text{units of } \frac{F_T}{\mu} = \frac{N}{kg/m} = \frac{kg \cdot m/s^2}{kg/m} = m^2/s^2$$

However, these are the units of speed squared! And the result is not only a proportionality, as we found above for frequency; it is also an equality. The speed of a traveling wave when the speed does not depend on the shape or the amplitude of the wave is:

$$v = \sqrt{\frac{F_T}{\mu}} = \sqrt{\frac{F_T}{M/L}} \qquad \textbf{speed of a traveling wave moving through a medium}$$

3.2.5 Interference between two traveling waves.
When two waves are moving toward each other, what happens when they are located at the same part of the string? We say that they *interfere*, and the way in which they interfere is relatively easy to describe and to apply. At each point along the medium, we simply add the contributions from each wave, keeping in mind that contributions can be negative, depending on the shape of the wave. In the following example, we show two waves interfering in three different ways. Note that in the region where the two waves overlap each other, the individual waves are shown as dotted lines. The sum of the two waves is shown as a solid line. This is what the string actually looks like at those instants of time.

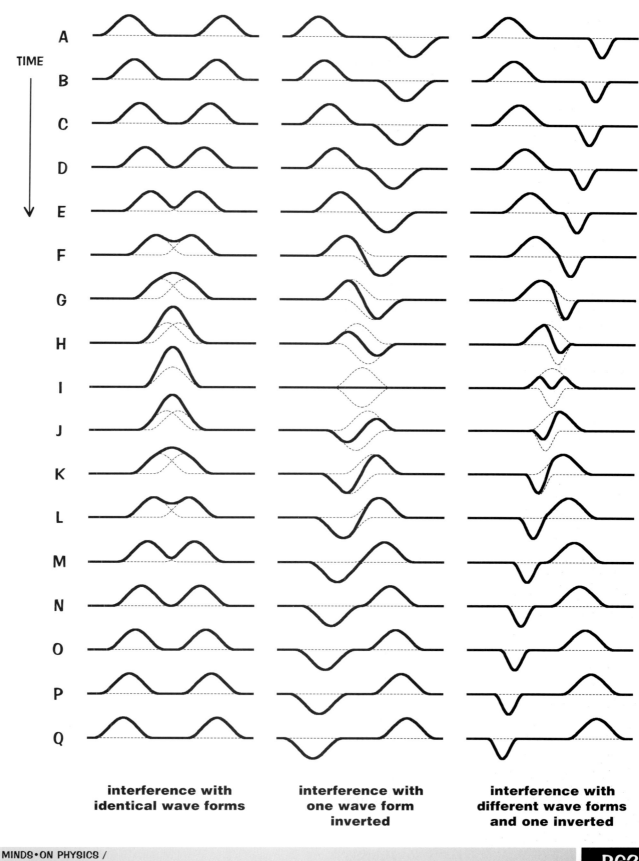

TIME

A

B

C

D

E

F

G

H

I

J

K

L

M

N

O

P

Q

**interference with
identical wave forms**

**interference with
one wave form
inverted**

**interference with
different wave forms
and one inverted**

The first column of diagrams shows the interference of two identical wave forms moving toward each other. At instant I, the peak of each one is at the middle of the string, and the result is a displacement twice as high as either one. After instant N, the waves no longer overlap, and they appear to continue on as if nothing happened.

However, it also might appear to you that the waves bounced off each other, like two carts hitting each other and returning to where they came from. The other two columns show how this is not the case. In the middle column, one of the waves consists of negative displacements while the other consists of positive displacements. When they interfere, their contributions partially or completely cancel each other out, so that at instants G, H, J, and K, the wave forms are smaller than either of the originals, and at I, there is no wave form there at all. But this does not mean that the situation is static. What is not shown is that the string is moving at instant I, which results in the observed behavior.

For some of you, it might appear again that the waves bounced off each other, with an inversion in between this time. In other words, you might think that the wave forms flip upon encountering one another. In the right column is shown the sequence of wave forms for waves of different shapes. After they interfere at instants G through K, they appear to continue on as though no interaction occurred. So, for all three cases, the waves behave as though they can pass through each other without interacting. The only observable effect is the shape of the string when the two waves are at the same location.

Interference is also useful for analyzing standing waves, because a standing wave may be thought of as two traveling waves of identical amplitude and speed moving in opposite directions. When they interfere, the characteristic nodes and oscillations occur.

3.2.6 Longitudinal vs. transverse waves. Earlier, we made a distinction between standing and traveling waves, and we have used examples of each type. The examples are also different in another respect. By comparing the direction of the displacement of the medium with the direction of the wave, we can distinguish waves from each other.

The wave moving through the five masses connected to springs is an example of a *longitudinal wave*, which occurs whenever the medium moves along the same axis as the direction of the wave. Sound waves are another example of a longitudinal wave because the motion of the molecules transmitting the sound is in the same direction as the direction of the wave.

The other two situations are examples of *transverse waves*, because the movement of the medium is perpendicular to the motion of the waves. For the vibrating guitar string, the waves are transverse because the directions of motion of the two traveling waves (left and right) is perpendicular to the displacement (or movement) of the string (i.e., up and down).

3.2.7 Reflection and transmission of traveling waves at an interface between two media.

When a wave is traveling along a string or other medium, energy is being transferred from one part of the string to the rest of it. When the string has an abrupt change of mass per unit length, we say that the wave hits an *interface* between two strings. When the wave hits this interface, some of its energy is transmitted to the new string and a new wave continues on in the same direction as before. Some of the energy is reflected, causing a third wave to begin traveling in the opposite direction. The characteristics of these two new waves depend on the relative masses per unit length of the two strings.

The sequences of drawings below show a wave hitting an interface for two different orientations of the string. The thicker string has the larger mass per unit length μ.

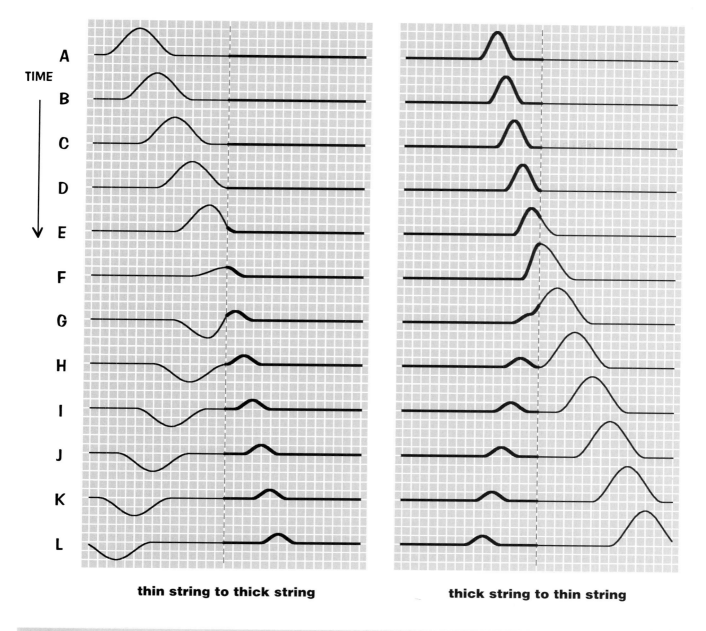

thin string to thick string   **thick string to thin string**

We can understand both of these sequences using force and impulse ideas. For the string on the left, the wave form starts in a thin string. When the front of the wave form hits the interface, the heavier string resists the force exerted by the light string, so it has a smaller amplitude than the incoming wave. The heavier string also delivers an impulse to the lighter string, causing it to invert. Both outgoing waves have smaller amplitudes than the incoming wave.

On the right side, the wave form starts in the heavier string. When it reaches the lighter string it delivers an upward impulse to the end of the string. Because the string is lighter, it reaches a larger maximum height than that of the incoming wave. The other outgoing wave has a smaller maximum height than that of the incoming wave.

Note that the speed of the wave is a property of the medium, not the circumstances. In the heavier medium the speed is always slower, because μ is larger there. It does not matter where the wave starts or which direction it is traveling. Also, the wave form always has a narrower width in the heavier medium, because the speed of the wave is smaller there.

3.2.8 Reflection of waves at a boundary. The limiting case of a wave hitting an interface occurs when one end of the string is held fixed, such as when the string is attached to a wall. The result is identical to the case in which the string is attached to a medium with very large mass per unit length: (1) There is no transmission of the wave, so the reflected wave has the same amplitude as the original wave; (2) The wave is hitting an interface with a higher mass per unit length, so the reflected wave is inverted. The diagram on the next page shows what happens when a wave hits a wall.

Instants A through D show the wave traveling to the right. At D, the leading edge of the wave hits the boundary. At E, we see that the part of the string attached to the wall is no longer horizontal, which means that the wall is delivering a vertical impulse to the string. This causes the wave form to collapse (F–H) eventually becoming flat (I). However, the string is not at rest, otherwise it would stay flat at all times. Parts of the string near the wall are moving downward, which causes the process described above to reverse itself. Now the wall delivers an upward impulse on the string until instant N, when the original wave form reappears—inverted and moving to the left—but the same shape as before. Instants N through Q show the inverted wave form continuing to travel to the left.

This completes the volume on complex systems. We hope you have seen how the behavior of many multi-particle systems—whether it is a fluid moving through a pipe, a gas being compressed or expanded, or a wave traveling along a string—can be analyzed, explained, and understood using the same physics concepts as before: forces, acceleration, momentum, impulse, work, kinetic energy, and potential energy.

WALL

TIME

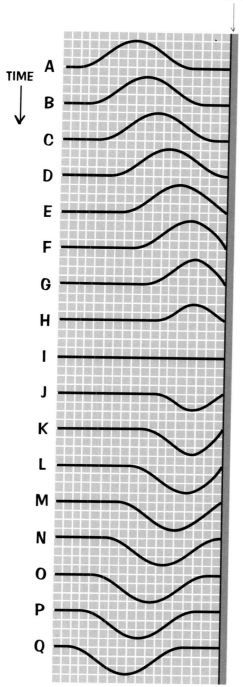

A
B
C
D
E
F
G
H
I
J
K
L
M
N
O
P
Q